Praise for *Weaving Dreams*

"Tami Longaberger has written a joyful, commonsense book which should be read in these uncommon times. She finds her roots in rural Ohio and draws on the wisdom of those roots and of her father, a true Horatio Alger character. This book will assure you that our best days are ahead of us."

—E. Gordon Gee
President, The Ohio State University

"Tami has captured the essence of leadership! She has the unique ability to inspire and share her passion for her company and its employees. Tami's principles apply to everyday life and when applied to business these tested principles will lead to success. *Weaving Dreams: The Joy of Work, The Love of Life* is beautifully written from her heart and filled with useful ideas for a lifetime."

—Georgette Mosbacher
President and CEO
Borghese, Inc.

"Tami weaves a basket full of personal stories and business insights to inspire us all to do our best. Using beautifully written 'family' stories, Tami Longaberger both instructs and inspires as she shares wisdom, insights, love, and encouragement for all humanity. Through trials and tribulations, sharing lessons learned, and showing how we can meet the challenges in our lives, *Weaving Dreams* is a candid account of a unique company and an extraordinary woman."

—Hope Taft
First Lady of Ohio Emeritus 1999–2007

"*Weaving Dreams: The Joy of Work, The Love of Life* tells a wonderful story of the history of the Longaberger family, the culture and character of the company whose handwoven baskets enrich thousands of homes, and of its chairman and CEO, Tami Longaberger, who helped build its success. It inspires and challenges the reader to think about the principles and people who have shaped their work and life, as well as the contributions they could make so others can achieve the American Dream."

—Jo Ann Davidson
Former Speaker of the House, State of Ohio
Former Co-Chair of the Republican National
Committee

"An intimate journey into a compelling, creative, and attractive personality that unravels and shares the threads which make up the vibrant tapestry of her life and success. A must read for those who seek the inspiration to take charge of their lives and achieve their dreams."

—**Sheri L. Orlowitz**
Entrepreneur and Founder of the Orlowitz-Lee
Children's Advocacy Center
Former Member of the National Women's Business Council

"*Weaving Dreams* is a beautiful collection of inspiring, heartfelt stories that connects us to real and intimate moments along Tami Longaberger's journey. Her experiences are so familiar that readers can genuinely feel the heart of a 'small town girl' with deep-rooted family values woven throughout the multiplicity of life's responsibilities as daughter, friend, mother, and corporate executive. These passionate stories ground us by reconnecting with the simple that matters most.

As readers, we gain a depth of understanding and appreciation into the heart of a strong, influential, and inspiring American woman and business leader. Tami's grace, elegance, and love for family, friends, and community are the spokes that bind her essence. We are left feeling fulfilled and inspired to find our own inner strength, to connect with others, and to appreciate all that surrounds us."

—**Lori Walker**
Head Women's Soccer Coach
The Ohio State University

"I am one of Tami's many admirers—not only because she practices one of my mother's pearls of wisdom: '*Work is a privilege*,' but she also understands that success is built on integrity and relationships. Tami has spent her life putting this into practice, and The Longaberger Company, along with her family and friends, has reaped the benefits. I recommend *Weaving Dreams* to the young entrepreneur as well as my family and friends. Tami's work is an inspiration and guide to anyone who possesses the courage to dream!"

—**The Honorable Bonnie McElveen Hunter**
Former Ambassador to Finland
Chair of the Board, The American Red Cross

weaving DREAMS

weaving
DREAMS

The Joy of Work, The Love of Life

Tami Longaberger

WILEY

John Wiley & Sons, Inc.

Published by John Wiley & Sons, Inc., Hoboken, New Jersey.

Published simultaneously in Canada.

For general information on our other products and services or for technical support, please contact our Customer Care Department within the United States at (800) 762-2974, outside the United States at (317) 572-3993 or fax (317) 572-4002.

Wiley also publishes its books in a variety of electronic formats. Some content that appears in print may not be available in electronic books. For more information about Wiley products, visit our web site at www.wiley.com.

Library of Congress Cataloging-in-Publication Data:

Longaberger, Tami, 1961-
   Weaving dreams: the joy of work, the love of life/Tami Longaberger.
     p. cm.
   ISBN 978-0-470-63003-7 (hardback); ISBN 978-0-470-92588-4 (ebk);
   ISBN 978-0-470-92589-2 (ebk); ISBN 978-0-470-92590-6 (ebk)
  1. Success in business. 2. Quality of life. 3. Corporate culture.
  4. Longaberger Company. 5. Longaberger, Tami, 1961- I. Title.
   HF5386.L768 2010
   658–dc22
                                       2010021339

Printed in the United States of America

10 9 8 7 6 5 4 3 2 1

This book is dedicated to

*The Women of the World: in honor of their tireless pursuit
to uncover the best in themselves. And once their best self is
found and realized, for the difference they strive to make in this
world, one life at a time: as mothers, daughters, sisters, and friends;
as businesswomen and community leaders; and ultimately,
as powerful catalysts for change.*

CONTENTS

Contents

FOREWORD

For years I ran and scrambled as a quarterback for the Cleveland Browns in the National Football League, throwing touchdowns and huddling up with men who shared an intense drive to be successful on the field—to not only win, but to be *the best*. To us this drive felt like a gnawing, unfed hunger rumbling in our bellies—a constant companion never allowing us to rest on our laurels. Instead, it picked away at us, pushing us to excel.

When I first met Tami, I saw that same drive alive in her. I recognized the fire in her eyes and the passion in her heart, and knew that she was not someone who would find satisfaction in anything less than her best. It drew me to her; that determination and laser focus.

At the same time, I quickly came to know her as a woman of great compassion and true humility. If ever she had a moment to stop and encourage someone or delay her own plans so that she could stop and sign a basket, she would do it. And nearly to a fault, if ever a spotlight was shining, she would steer it away from herself, finding another to share in the glory and applause. She embodies "team player" in all the right and most honorable ways.

Tami seems to effortlessly walk the delicate tightrope of business and *woman*. In one instant she makes decisions with the potential to impact the lives of hundreds or possibly thousands of people dependent upon this company called *Longaberger*. And in the next—she is at home, arranging flowers, spending time with her children, and sending handwritten notes to those whom she loves and appreciates.

Perfecting this kind of effort is so rare that even my children have taken notice of Tami's gift of balance and even-handedness. And at this stage in my life, it strikes me as being a matter of unparalleled good fortune that they have her example to watch and learn from. This is particularly true with my oldest two daughters, aged seventeen and eighteen. In the midst of their busy teenage lives, they pause, now, to see a woman exemplifying success, confidence, and intelligence, and recognize that Tami has proven that it is possible for a woman to achieve—*and have it all.*

Rather than wilting to the world's ideals for women that place such inordinate value on what you look like or who you know—or whether you can secure a relationship that will provide financial security and worldly comforts—Tami proves that there is more. Instead of worming under the boot of obligation and dependence, Tami demonstrates that women can rise above, embodying independence and strength. Instead of stifling growth by settling for *just okay,* she summons them to break through brittle shells that confine and strip away dreams.

In short, Tami conveys—not just through words, but *by her actions*—that women who are willing to work hard, who hope and toil to reach their goals, *can actually realize them.*

This kind of thinking has overturned the way I think about women and about the pathways each woman must carve out for herself. For so long I was not used to seeing independent, self-supportive women who could—and who *wanted to*—be their own person. The women I knew were often content to let their identity intertwine so profoundly with another person or social status, that true self-esteem was never developed.

I can now see how the slope quickly grows dangerous and slippery for young women in particular. I understand how it takes away hopes and a sense of imagination when planning for the future. Being content to coast along under the umbrella of another, *while not wrong*, can curdle the cream as it rises to the top.

And so, meeting Tami and participating fully in her life has not only been a beacon of fresh perspective for me and for so many others; it has changed the lens through which I view women while also informing my parenting. Like many of you, I want only the best for my children: I long for them to see the gleam of their own faces reflecting back from shiny and bright futures. And part of that gleam, I'm convinced, will spring from what I've learned from this incredible woman.

Weaving Dreams: The Joy of Work, The Love of Life is a collection of Tami's most treasured and heartfelt stories and life-lessons. It contains memories from her childhood, memories of her father, and memories of mothering her own children. It shares the journeys of several other amazing women who overcame great odds—if even by overcoming their own doubts—to evolve into people they never thought they could be. Maybe you'll see a shadow of yourself in them?

As a man, I feel so privileged to have been able to join Tami on part of her life journey. And because she has impacted my life so drastically—and because I've learned so much from her, I truly feel that this book will be deemed an important resource for *men as well as women*. I realize now that it is equally vital for men to recognize the strength of authentic femininity—the strength that comes with uncovering your true self and removing the tethers of a society, world, or social setting that would hold you back.

So wherever you are in life, it is my hope that you would be empowered as you read. And if this book impacts you at all, *pay it forward.* Who knows? What you read here might be just the thing that your sister, brother, or friend needs to hear.

Thanks for Reading,

Bernie J. Kosar

ACKNOWLEDGMENTS

First, always, I would like to thank my family:

Claire and Matthew: You have infused my life with such immense joy and changed me forever, for the better. I am so proud to be your mom.

Bernie: For all the listening and compassion you are quick to offer; you bring love, friendship, and happiness into my world each day.

My Dad Dave, my Mother Laura and her husband Jim, my Sister Rachel and her husband Todd, and their children Kaitlin, Dustin, Benjamin, Rose, Isabelle, and John Todd: Your support and encouragement have an immeasurable impact on me.

Bob Dilenschneider and Joe Tessitore: Thank you for helping make this book—this dream—a reality.

Richard Narramore and the folks at John Wiley & Sons, Inc.: For the vision you cast, for shaping raw ideas and broad topics into something exciting and compelling.

Jane Graham: For listening to my stories and helping me find the right words.

The Entire Longaberger Family of Sales Associates and Employees: You will always be family to me.

Part 1
America

1 Love Where You Live

Finding Joy at Home

I can't say for certain exactly how it happened, or when; but like a slow marinade of spices and oils and herbs, my body has been soaking in the Midwest since my mother first wrapped me in a white blanket. I have absorbed the textures unique to each season: Lush grasses upholstering rolling hills, the crunch of leaves underfoot as I scout goldfinches in the garden. I have listened to the winter calls of red-tailed hawks that fly boldly near the icy, spring-fed waters of our pond. I have memorized the lines and arches of the trees I love, stared in reverence as they swayed in the wind, bending and dancing and nearly singing to me—composing a forest cathedral that seemed to be mine alone.

I know this place as one knows a sister or a close friend—intimately and effortlessly.

Trying to remove the Midwest from my being—from my blood—would be akin to attempting to separate out the varied ingredients in my mom's winter potato soup: *Impossible*. My love for this place is so ingrained in me—so deeply pressed upon my very soul—that it is part-and-parcel of *who I am*.

I remember a day when I was a child, bouncing along in the backseat of my grandparents' Buick on our way to Amish Country. I always loved those Sunday drives; hearing the gravel crunch on the old country roads, driving somewhere to pick wildflowers on a hill or in a meadow. The autumn sun streamed in through half-open windows and dust danced in the glow of the backseat as I watched barns flash before me like immense wooden strawberries on county-sized vines.

Maybe that's the first time I paid attention to Ohio; maybe that's the first time I knew it was special to me. Or to someone.

Living here has, in some ways, softened me—to the beauty of the earth and the simplicity of nature. Yet in other ways, it has toughened me—left me with calloused hands and skinned knees. I hold both sides of the coin in my hands, feeling the weight equally.

It hasn't always been easy to live in a small town with a big last name, so my dad made sure I observed and *practiced* the Midwest work ethic that makes us the "Breadbasket of America." After all, if we're going to feed the nation, we must all be ready to get some dirt under our nails.

Midwesterners, I've found, are ready to do that hard work. Whether it's farming or manufacturing, our state stands on the shoulders of willing workers and their desire to make honorable contributions to society. I grew up seeing that—not only from my mother and father—but from neighbors and teachers and friends; people who ask for honest pay for an honest day's work. People who find pride and esteem in holding a job that provides for their families. Ohioans, it seems, embody the Midwest work ethic that epitomizes Longaberger—and, in a greater sense, the history of basket weaving in America.

In light of these willing hands and able bodies, I can't tell you how acutely I feel the pain that accompanies the dismantling of so many jobs across our nation and even more so here, closer to home. To recognize that people want to be given a chance—just *one shot* at a better life—and to see them stumble over shoestrings that someone else untied is sometimes more than I can bear. I turn on the news and see that faces are cast down while unemployment numbers are steadily up. Sadly, we no longer live in a time of abundant factory jobs and blue-collar opportunities. And there are times during quiet moments when I wonder: *What if my dad were trying to start this business now—in 2010? Could he do it? Would it thrive? . . . Would it even survive?*

There are people who look at me and consider my position within this company, assuming that I "have it made." *Why would Tami have to worry?* they might wonder. Well, believe me—I worry *plenty!* I worry about the employees who depend on me. I worry about treating them fairly and balancing their needs with an ever-present bottom line. I worry about keeping this tradition alive—about developing another generation of first-class basket weavers who will find an audience in the marketplace and esteem in the town square. I worry about the Midwest.

But amidst these ominous gray clouds, rays of light splinter and break their way through the bleak exterior. If you're willing to wait and watch, you'll see them, too. It seems to me that taking a step back lends a new perspective to these clouds. Maybe it requires taking a deep breath and going back to school to find your light. Maybe it means taking a step in a totally different direction, while capturing a willingness to try new things that you never imagined doing.

For me, the light comes when I take a step across the ocean.

I have been blessed with opportunities to serve women on the global stage, and proudly serve as the chair of the Arab Women Leadership Institute. As such, I was honored with an invitation to travel to Jordan as one of my biannual trips. Nestled between

Israel and Saudi Arabia, Jordan is a land peacefully tangled in a complex history. Although women are well represented in their universities, they are striving to move upward socially, sharing many of the dreams that you and I have for ourselves: To be respected, to make a difference, to achieve their own definition of success.

When I met Dr. Wajeeha Sadiq Al-Baharna, I knew I had encountered a strong and interesting individual who was destined to make waves in her country. An expert in interpreting women's rights in the Koran, Dr. Wajeeha explained to me that the Koran *does not* place upon women the kinds of heavy restrictions and legalism that we see marching across our TV screens on the evening news. Rather, she argues, men have *distorted* the guidelines in this book and imposed these rules as a form of religious fanaticism. Dr. Wajeeha dreams of helping women inch forward in their fight for equality, and she is willing to step outside of very structured boxes to do that.

Dr. Wajeeha could very well leave the land she loves; she could look out at the burkas and list off the rules and say, *Never mind! It's not worth the fight!* And I can't say I would blame her if she chose that path. Transforming the perceptions and beliefs of a community—an entire culture—is a *monumental task.*

But Dr. Wajeeha isn't choosing that path. Instead of giving up and walking away in defeat, Dr. Wajeeha *stays* in her country, remains true to her homeland, and strives to make it better.

And isn't that what so many of us have done in these tough economic times? Of course, some families have had to move by necessity—and justifiably so. However, I seem to hear about just as many who have stayed and tried to move mountains in the communities where they've grown up and come to love.

Take a moment and reflect on your own journey over the past year or two. Have there been moments when leaving the place you call home seemed particularly tempting? If you decided against the move, what was it that held you in place? Was it family? Your church or religious community? The landscape and the beauty that has become like an old friend?

And if you had to move, do you ever think about home? What do you miss? What do you love about your new surroundings? How can you bring fresh light to that place?

Wherever the road of life has taken you, I'm certain if you search your memories that you will find that the geography of your childhood has made a few cameo appearances. Perhaps the landscape was one of the characters in your story; maybe it even had the starring role. For many, visiting the beach in summer is so intertwined with thoughts of mom and dad that they're pressed to remember family without sand and water and pails of shells.

That's the beauty of *place*—the beauty of *home.* It becomes a part of you even when you move and try to stuff it away; even when you don't realize you're soaking it in, there you are, heart and soul, *marinating.*

Whether I'm working with Arab women or European business women or the Ambassador for Kenya, I look into eyes eager for direction and creative ideas . . . and I see light. I see the spark of ingenuity that I see in America, and it reminds me of home.

The home I love, that continues to shape me and inform my worldview.

The home that gives me hope and light for the future.

2 Only in America

Seizing Opportunities and Finding Silver Linings

I was born in the fall of 1961 in the foothills of Ohio's Appalachian Mountains. My mother had spent the day with a number two pencil, filling in row upon row of multiple-choice questions on her Nursing Boards Exam, only to return home and fill the air with the kind of heaving screams that bring new life into the world. It was October 20—and the beginning of everything.

As poor timing would have it, my father had been drafted to serve in the U.S. Army's effort in the Berlin Crisis of 1961, effectively leaving my mother to be a single mom struggling against the unrelenting poverty that strangles Appalachia to this day. Rather than staying in our little house alone, she packed up our few belongings and escaped to the comfort of my grandmother's home.

I use the word "comfort" here relatively. True: It was a comfort for my mom to have an extra pair of hands to help wash me and prepare dinner. It was a comfort to have another voice to echo hers and a mother's wisdom surrounding her, rather than the lonely sound of solitude that rings like thunder when your body aches for company. But *comfort* did not include the modern conveniences we've come to expect in this country.

Even in 1961, my grandparents, Ula Mae and William Herman Eschman—and by extension *all of us*—were living in a small wooden home with an outhouse and no running water. A hot bath meant boiling pan after pan of creek water and letting it splash into a metal tub on the kitchen floor. A trip to the bathroom after dark meant tiptoeing through brambles and over tree roots before shutting the door on your closet-sized destination. It was the comfort of kin over convenience; the comfort of mother and tender hand that drew my mom back to her homestead.

And so—like countless others before me in Ohio and Kentucky, West Virginia and Tennessee—my journey of life started as a baby held in the balance of Appalachia.

With time comes a certain perspective that allows us to more accurately weigh the gravity of our beginnings. And what keeps coming back to me in greater wonderment each time is the thought that I started my life in a place *without running water*. Yet now, by the grace of God, I find myself living a full and amazing life beyond anything I could have ever dreamed. *Only in America* could a girl like me find such opportunity and seize it, turning it over and over until it became the smooth likeness of a dream.

I've been blessed to see my children grow and learn the value of hard work. I've worked with U.S. and foreign presidents, kings and princes, princesses, and cardinals from Rome. I've seen our company grow and give men and women opportunities to reach for bigger dreams and farther horizons.

And while it's true that I have been blessed immeasurably, it has not come without exhausting, costly work. I've been in the trenches, so to speak, for years—learning and earning my way through this company, and I have to admit that there have been times when moving forward seemed impossible. When giving up would have made sense. It would have been justifiable. But it would not be accepted—not by us, and not by me.

In 1986 the Longaberger Company faced a seemingly insurmountable debt load of $7 million. After Dad confided in Rachel and me that he was going to call it quits in the face of such a trial, we convinced him to do *anything he could* to save the business. Dad put it all on the line: he laid off over 900 Basketmakers, imposed pay cuts on those remaining, stripped our product line down, and raised prices on everything else.

Those were terrible years for all of us. In a small community like Dresden, letting go of 900 decent, quality workers made the clouds sink a little closer to earth; everything seemed gray that year. And although we were able to pull out of that murky abyss, we did so with battle scars I still carry.

In late 1997, my father was diagnosed with renal cell cancer. By March 1999, he was dead. Rachel and I felt our hearts splay open and be laid bare before us. No one expects to lose a father who's only 62 years old. And when you do, few can truly anticipate the undertow that grabs you and sucks you down, pinning you underwater when all you want is the sun.

Before the veil of tears could be lifted and dried after my father's death, I was doubled over and writhing from the pain of divorce. Two devastating blows dealt to me within three weeks of each other left me limping and gasping for air.

At the end of March that year, an imposing corporate desk and shoes I never intended to fill sat empty and waiting for me in Newark, Ohio. A home, now broken, left sharp edges and unfamiliar fissures for me to navigate unwittingly. I could barely find my footing, much less think like the "visionary" Longaberger needed me to be as we embarked on this new chapter in our short history. All the while, the line of employees with questions and concerns and deadlines lined the hallway outside my office door like dominoes waiting to fall.

And all the while, I was dying inside. Unable to grieve. Unable to fill my lungs with enough air. Unable to sit in the stillness and let my eyes cough up torrents of tears and heartbreak.

Instead, piles of work sat before me. Papers to sign. Arrangements to make. Meetings and payroll and . . . emptiness.

Do not be fooled into believing that sitting at this desk has been filled with only lollipops and rainbows, or baskets of tulips and daffodils, for that matter. I promise you that while sitting here is indeed a tremendous blessing, this desk still casts shadows when the lights go out.

The silver lining in all of this pain, however, was coming to the realization that I can wake up to a new day. And even though some wounds never heal completely, the scab starts to dry, and the scar diminishes. And with a little love and tenderness, the silver lining gives way to a radiant sunset that seems—at least in that moment—to redeem part of what was lost.

We in America have been granted the unbelievable opportunity to search for silver linings every day. In the great expanse of this country, I truly believe that you can do *whatever you set out to do*—as long as you get up every day and *keep trying*. It's possible! Who would have ever dreamed that my dad—a poor boy in the early part of this century—would have made a living at weaving baskets . . . let alone build a company that would go on to employ over 8,000 people? Who would have thought that in less than 50 years, I could go from a baby in an Appalachian cottage to CEO of this company? But in America, it's possible. In America, *your dreams* are possible.

At Longaberger, we like to tell women that they can achieve *their own "American Dream."* And one of the shining joys of my job is getting to see women whose lives are changed because of their determined efforts to find that dream and call it into reality. When I meet a consultant whose life has been revitalized or transformed by the opportunity Longaberger gives them, my spirit floats. It is such a magical thing that women who perhaps did not previously fully grasp their innate, raw power are now stretching to their full potential.

Ann Doty of Alaska is one of those women. Her story is inspiring, not just because she's a Branch Leader and a breast cancer survivor—but because she has named and claimed her own silver lining. She has chased her American Dream and *found it*.

As Ann recently told me, "When I first started with Longaberger, I was hoping to add a few baskets to my collection and maybe make a few new friends." She thought maybe she'd stick with it for a few years, reach her goals, make a little extra money, and then retire with her husband and enjoy the beauty of Juneau. Fourteen years and over *six hundred* baskets later—not including those on her boat or in the RV—she is still with the company, leading and mentoring 23 other women who have become like family to her. Those women look up to her as they define their American Dream and look for their own silver linings. And Ann couldn't be happier to help them on their way.

Ann tells me she has found enrichment, confidence, and a new identity with Longaberger. And although she has earned baskets and cruises and extra income, none of these, she says, compares to the warm sense of family that encourages her to meet and exceed goals. She explains that the motivation to become the best you can be increases momentum like "a runaway train." If you want to go for it, Longaberger will give you the legroom to try. Ann has tried, and she has succeeded—while inspiring so many other women to continue reaching and dreaming.

As I grow older, I realize more and more how much this country means to me, and how much I treasure the opportunities found within its borders. I love this indescribable expanse called the United States of America—this land that allows us all to stretch and grow and dance. Each day, as I soak in my surroundings—as I continue to become more attuned to the importance of *place* and *home* and *roots*—something whispers to me. I lean closer and hear my heart tell me, *"You are so blessed to be American. To enjoy the freedoms you nearly take for granted. To have built a life here from your own hard work and from the hard work of those who have gone before you. Treasure it."*

And so I ask you: What are your hopes and aspirations? What kind of legacy do you want to leave for your children? We've all read the poem that promises that in a hundred years, we won't care about the size of our bank accounts or the kind of car we drive—and that may be true. But what about five years from now? Or ten? What is *your* silver lining?

I challenge you to seize the opportunity that America lends you. Grab hold of your life and live it out as one squeezing the last drops of sweet juice from summer fruit. There are very few places where—simply by virtue of geography—you are given a blank canvas to paint with the brilliance and gusto of your hours and minutes. Efforts and ideas unique to you. Creativity unleashed in a flurry of red, white, and blue.

America has handed you the palate and the brush. Get started on your own American Dream.

3 Lessons from Purple Hands

Learning Work Ethic from My Father

I can remember as a very young child standing in quiet shadows, watching my grandfather stand bent over a basket out in the shop, work-worn hands fussing with splints of different colors and sizes. It was spring and he was intent on having a new batch ready for the waves of people planning after-church picnics on the fresh lawns and hillsides of Ohio. With an aching back and head hung low over his craft, minutes and hours were woven away in the chase for his American Dream.

Some of you may already know my Dad's story—of how he grew up learning the craft from his own father, my Grandpa J.W., who had made a living from baskets before the Great Depression laid on our country like a suffocating blanket. As the 5th of 12 children, Dad was a scrapper: Though he lived with epilepsy and stuttered, in those desperate times, all the Longaberger kids were expected to contribute to the household. Each day was a lesson in the classroom of life, and Dad quickly learned that nothing would be handed to him—that achieving what he wanted out of life would demand constant work and tireless effort.

It was the early 1970s when Dad pitched the idea of selling Grandpa's baskets, and J.W. thought the concept was a bit far-fetched. Despite the fact that my father had proven himself as a fantastic salesman in his grocery store, restaurant, and drug store, Grandpa insisted that nobody in Dresden would pay more than $1.50 for a basket.

But Dad proved him wrong. The baskets sold for $5 apiece.

My father's journey toward his dream was fraught with heartache, sweat, and uncertainty, commingled with dogged determination and unflinching tenacity. I look back on those early years and remember how it felt for me as a teenage girl—and the emotion that keeps bubbling up to the surface is *confusion. Why was Dad such a nonconformist? Why did he insist on taking the hard way? Why did we have to stand out?* Though I didn't ask these questions aloud, answers rang back in deafening fashion via my father's work ethic and belief in pulling yourself up by your bootstraps.

Then, in 1975, Dad introduced me to my own.

When I was 14 years old—when the rest of my friends were still swooning over Greg Brady and David Cassidy—my Dad announced in no uncertain terms that I needed to get a job.

"That's it!" he declared. "You're going to work!" He marched me over to his little restaurant where I was positioned as a Sunday hostess. In addition to helping seat people, I was expected to wait tables. Let me tell you—that experience gave me a new respect and appreciation for what servers endure. From cranky customers to heavy trays of food bustled around on aching feet, I have never forgotten how difficult that job was for me. To this day, when I go into a restaurant, I do my best to be pleasant and generous, tipping extra and being complimentary—all because of what I learned at 14.

Well, the restaurant job ended after two weeks, with my father agreeing with my estimation that it simply was "not a good fit." Everyone has their own toolboxes filled with

God-given tools—and mine simply did not include those needed for food services! We decided that Dad's grocery store might better suit me; so off I went to stock shelves, spraying blue ink on old stampers, rolling a fair price across the face of each can, and returning home with purple hands. Each Wednesday night was the same routine: Price the merchandise, slide the old to the front, and sneak the new in the back.

Blue spray, purple hands.

The funny thing about purple hands is that they tend to stare back at you, in an almost mocking way. Others notice them. They are difficult to hide and hard to clean. Yet now, with years on my side—and the wisdom that accompanies them—I can see that my purple hands were a badge of pride. They showed the world that I worked with my hands; that they did more than brush through my hair or fluff dreamy pillows. My hands worked *hard*. Staring at the purple reminded me that as a Longaberger, *nothing* was *given; everything* had to be *earned*.

While I'll admit to you now that those hands were a working girl's badge, getting me out the door to go to work was a job in and of itself. My Dad would shake his head in frustration at my obstinacy, probably recognizing the fighter in me as a mirror image of himself. Yet, as if a switch was flipped, once I got to work, I truly enjoyed it. And even though I didn't intentionally adjust my attitude in either direction, Dad joked that I "turned on the charm" around customers. I like to think that I was finding my niche in listening to others, finding joy in treating them right, helping them locate items, and building rapport with the members of our little village.

That desire to please and work hard only intensified as my 16th birthday approached and I had my eye on a sweet little green 1973 stick shift Mercury hatchback. I have to laugh when I look back: Why in heaven did I need a vehicle when I lived in a town of

1,200 people situated on all of 10 city blocks? I guess when you're 16, *you just do.*

Dad promised that he'd make the down payment for me, but I'd have to come up with the rest. I never knew how much $85 a month was when measured with hours in a store and purple ink on my hands. I never knew how long it would take to accumulate the $110 for insurance or pay for the weekly trips to the gas station just so I could drive the short distance to Zanesville with my girlfriends on the weekend.

I also never knew how this experience would shape me. Could my father have offered to buy that car outright for me? Probably. Could he have slipped me a few extra bucks every week for gas? Or surprised me by taking it and filling it up himself? Sure. But to my Dad, this was a moment ripe for teaching—a time for me to learn the realities of money management and work and profit and sacrifice. Buying my first car and making monthly payments on it rather than slurping down my paycheck at the soda fountain gave me some valuable parameters for life. I didn't like it at the time, but then again, growing in discipline and responsibility isn't usually the hallmark for many teenagers, anyway.

My father was—still is—a giant in my eyes. The space he occupies in my heart still pushes it to new limits. I hear his voice and feel his eyes upon me as I work and anguish over tough decisions. And every time I put on my boots to go out to my barn or wander over the soil of home, it reminds me that this world—this life—is mine for the making. It's up to me. I have to claim each day—seize it for good and determine to be productive.

It's the Longaberger way. This dream, however wonderful, does not come without effort.

I'm so glad my Dad prepared me for it.

I'm so grateful for purple hands.

4 With Feet Planted

Learning Respect for Our Country

If I'm being honest, I'll admit that my respect for this nation took root in the middle of a gymnasium before a high school basketball game.

My Dad, in his famously "subtle" style, let me know in no uncertain terms that I was to stand at attention during the singing of "The Star Spangled Banner," paying respect to those men and women who wore their uniforms proudly in defense of our country.

"Never let me see you move during the National Anthem," he hissed, finger to my face. Looking into those dark eyes, I knew I'd better plant my feet and get serious. No gum snapping. No hair twirling. No checking the time on the clock or staring at the cute boy from Algebra class. Because somewhere, somehow—Dad *was watching.*

In my estimation, the marrow in the bones of the average Midwesterner holds a deep, long-standing sense of patriotism. They possess a solid and unwavering love for this country and what it stands for: Hard work, freedom, human ingenuity, courage, innovation, dreams, and endless possibilities. The people who have moved in and out of our story have modeled that kind of devotion time and time again, influencing my father from his childhood. The summer he was drafted was one of pride and honor for him, accompanied, certainly, with a measure of fear. Serving our country was seen as a duty to country.

In December of 1961, my Dad came home on leave from his tour of duty during the Berlin Crisis. He swooped me up and carried our family to Fort Hood, Texas, where we lived in military housing for the next several months. Although I was too young to remember the feeling of the Texas dirt or the smell of the heat on pavement, I know now that those years added a web of twisting roots to an already–firmly planted affection for our nation.

My Dad came to more fully appreciate the gravity of the sacrifice that so many before him had made. He saw each day how families rearranged their lives to serve and live on the base; how they gave up the proximity of family and the landscape of home. And I think Dad realized in a new way how precisely our country relied on thousands of willing soldiers to protect its borders, its future, and our values. He was honored to be one of them.

After military life, my father carried his love of country with him into the daily routines that seemed mundane. From turning the key on his little restaurant door to ringing up sales in the grocery store, Dad breathed patriotism. As he moved through life and eventually returned to the American craft of his heritage, he felt that love more than ever, raising Rachel and me to live under the banner of fidelity to America.

Because of the kind of person my Dad was and the kind of company he wanted Longaberger to be, we're delighted to continue to pay tribute to our men and women in uniform, in addition to the veterans who we employ. It has been my distinct privilege to get to know so many of our Longaberger vets; their stories inspire and embolden us to fly our flags proudly.

Branch leader Billie Anderson of Salt Lake City has one of my favorite wartime stories; hearing her account forced me to slow down and take notice, affecting me in ways I wasn't expecting. Billie started with our company in 1989, 10 years after returning to active duty with the Army. She served in Operation Desert Shield on the Kuwaiti border in the first Iraq war and was separated from husband, children, and home for several months.

Pitching a tent in shifting sand provided a powerful metaphor for Billie: Things were changing. Life there was unsteady. This was not the lush, green home they all knew and loved and missed. Instead, they felt pulled up by the roots, transplanted carelessly as if a new gardener hastily planted daisies in wet clay. They did not belong there, but for that season, the unforgiving sands of the desert were to be home. And they knew they had to do their best not to choke on the storms or drown in the clay.

Surrounded by other troops who were equally unmoored and longing for a piece of home—a snatch of Americana—an idea sparked in Billie's mind. *Why not have a Longaberger party right here? Why not remind my friends of home and dreams and a better life?*

When the photo came in the mail, I called Billie immediately. Ten people knelt in desert sand *wearing gas masks* to preserve safe breathing, holding Longaberger catalogs and Wish Lists victoriously, as though they proclaimed to the world, *"We have not forgotten our homeland!"*

You can't imagine the geyser of emotion fighting to escape when I looked upon each one of those faces—unknown, yet beloved—staring back from a moment frozen in time; a moment now melting my heart an ocean away. How can I arrange words on a page to convey how humbled I felt? How can I locate the sentiment and capture it here when the only thing that rises to the surface are tears? To think that our company and our baskets brought a bit of relief to hurting hearts in Kuwait—or that a Longaberger gathering would be the balm to get someone past the next mental or emotional hurdle—is amazing. And it *quiets* me.

What can we, as a company, do to reflect our gratitude? How can we best support the lofty sacrifices that our military personnel make each day?

For one thing, we make sure that their families continue to receive insurance. We are flexible—we keep their jobs waiting for them. We hang up photos and proudly display the names of those serving. We bring them onto the stage at our yearly convention in Ohio called "The Bee."

We applaud, cheer, and honor them daily. Because that's what Longaberger is all about.

I am so proud of the partnership we have built with one of our employees, Kristen Wenrick, over the past few years. Kristen, who's currently active with the Ohio Air National Guard, joined The Longaberger Company in 2006 and has since been deployed overseas to Guam. In addition to her foreign deployments, Kristen has had several stateside stints for Officer's Training as she was promoted to Second Lieutenant. [*Hooray, Kristen!*]

During Kristen's time of service, Longaberger worked diligently to accommodate her needs and honor her commitment to the Guard by offering differential pay to supplement military pay. While she was gone from our midst, it was my great personal pleasure to write to her words of encouragement, motivating her in her pursuit of excellence. And I was a proud cheerleader when I learned that many of Kristen's Longaberger co-workers had assembled care packages filled with gifts and treats and letters to a far-off friend.

To us, making an effort in these small areas is simply the right thing to do. To our great joy and surprise, at the completion of

Kristen's deployments, Longaberger was awarded the Patriot Award for extending outstanding support during military service. Wow. I never imagined that *doing the right thing deserved an award,* but I guess these days it does.

I don't know if that makes me sad, or proud. Should I feel sad that honoring our military—which *everyone* should be doing— merited an award? On some levels it seems expected, ordinary, and, well, *required* of us all. A wonderful, rare, special *duty.*

But at the same time, I felt—and feel—*immensely* proud. Proud that honoring the military meant that Longaberger was recognized. Proud knowing that we not only did the expected, but that we exceeded it. We rose above the ordinary and the required and surpassed them both with our colors flying: red, white, and blue streaming in celebration.

That's a victory. *That's* patriotism.

And to me, that's just as important as not moving during the National Anthem.

5 A Pocket Full of Coins

Connecting with Bravery and Honor

On the sidewalks of U.S. cities—from Los Angeles to New York to San Antonio—masses of humanity pass each other, flash a smile, and continue on, heels click-clacking until the sound is swallowed up by the noise of the city. Walking into the distance, people disappear just like the smoke and exhaust coughed up by taxis and buses: out of your life in a second—if ever they were in it to begin with.

Sometimes I wonder about the people I pass. What's their destination? Who's waiting for them when they get there? What's life like in their shoes?

It's mind-boggling, when you take time to think about it, how we live parallel lives, occupying small squares of this globe, often never intersecting. We may exchange pleasantries and ask about vacation plans or deals at the market—but do we *really connect* anymore?

Perhaps you have heard about U.S. military coins; they originated in World War I when American volunteers from all over our country suited up for flying squadrons and pledged their lives for our country. As the story goes, a wealthy lieutenant had intricate bronze medallions embossed with his Marine Corps squadron's emblem, and kept them—one for each member of his squadron—close to his heart in a small leather pouch. With such a priceless symbol hanging at his chest, the lieutenant was alert and determined, buoyed by thoughts of those under his care.

One day the lieutenant's aircraft was badly damaged, forcing him to land behind German lines. Caught and stripped of all his possessions save the pouch of coins, he sat plotting and waiting for the perfect moment to flee. After a series of miraculously timed events, he successfully made his way to a French outpost where the coins were used to help identify him—thereby saving his life.

In honor of this lieutenant's bravery, our modern Marines also carry coins linking them to respective squadrons within the Corps. To anchor the tradition and ensure that soldiers have their coins on their person at all times, a challenge was born: One service member asks another to produce his or her coin at a local establishment. If this person cannot show his or her coin, they must buy a drink for the challenger. If the coin is shown, the Marine who asked to see it must buy.

These coins are a revered component of a Marine's uniform, a silent resident, if you will. Though hidden, they represent history and honor—a secret password known only to the men and women in uniform. Like the legendary lieutenant who went before them so many years ago, escaping with his life and his bag of medallions, our soldiers fiercely guard their coins, often saving them forever as a reminder of battles fought and time served.

Dog tags. Coins. Uniforms. Boots and helmet—the wardrobe of a soldier. They come together to write a sacred chapter in a person's life. It's often a chapter that goes on to define him or her, provide a lens for life, and lend a certain perspective on the world.

Although we cannot legally calculate a number, our estimates show that more than 15 percent of Longaberger extended family members are—or have a family member who is—actively serving in the U.S. military. Even as an estimate, that number makes me stop and take notice. That number makes me proud.

So when a soldier comes into my office donned in dress uniform, shoes polished and shined to match the gleam in his smile, I stand up. I feel honored that he would take the time to see me, granting me a place on his meager leave calendar.

Walking toward the center of the room, he extends his hand, as so many others have done. It meets mine in the stillness, and I immediately feel the weight of something hidden within our handshake. A new secret for us to share—something special for me to steward.

And all of a sudden, I realize . . . he has passed his coin to me. A piece of himself, a parcel of his identity—*gifted to me.*

I am blessed.

I am honored.

I am brought low.

And if you came into my office today, you would see that I have a growing collection of these precious symbols of service taking up residence around me; thirty-five small round reminders of the sweat and effort and dedication of so many souls.

I find it remarkable that—in a world where people hurry with their own agendas, plugged into a myriad of technological devices, bound by watch and planner and deadlines—these soldiers stop. They slow down. They unplug. And they *connect.* They reach out their hands and readily portion off their dearest possessions to one another. It's something we all desire to do on some level, and something that our company is incredibly proud to support.

We at Longaberger are glad to receive these coins. And just like the connections they represent, we promise to steward them to the best of our ability.

6 An American Privilege

Being a Voice for the Voiceless

One of the recent highlights of my life came in 2004, when a White House staffer called my office early in the day. To my surprise and delight, President George W. Bush was inviting me to serve on the Human Rights Commission that would be convening in Geneva, Switzerland, during March and April of that year.

For six weeks I was the only female U.S. delegate in attendance, sharing the stage with heroes and notable American figures. I was there with others like Louis Zuniga, a man who bravely opposed Castro's regime in Cuba and was repaid with 16 years in prison—13 of which were spent *in solitary confinement*. I met dignitaries, ambassadors, assistants to presidents, law professors, and Vietnam vets. It was a life-changing trip that continues to impact me deeply to this day.

The first time we walked into the giant oval embassy hall at The Palais des Nations, I felt as though I were Jonah being swallowed up by the whale—so small and overwhelmed by the size and history of this space. What an *honor* it was simply to be there! Making our way through aisles of connected tables and padded chairs, we approached the place where the U.S. delegates would be positioned. In front of each seat was a placard with the name of the country represented. It was a larger-than-life moment, so I sat down and took it all in. How proud I was to be a representative of the United States of America!

Moments later, as bodies began to stream into the hall and fill seats, I found myself spellbound by the variety of clothes and lovely variation in skin tones. Names now connected to faces. Faces from Latvia, Uganda, Italy, Ukraine—even the Holy See.

I felt as though the world itself was on display right in front of me. And it was magical.

We were often invited to embassy dinners for wine and food and company in the evenings after our meetings. As the only female U.S. delegate, I seemed to garner more than my share of invitations, even though I never went anywhere unattended. Those nights gave me pause to consider the vast range of accents, the flecks of color in the eyes of a new friend, the textures and patterns on fabric that was new and beautiful. The world seemed to crack open and give birth to a classroom of experiences just for me.

During one of those nights, I met Amina Mohamed, the Parliament Ambassador for Kenya. Dressed in a head-to-toe yellow print sprinkled with dark brown geometrical shapes, Ambassador Mohamed was a beam of light and kindness. I liked her immediately.

One day after our sessions, Ambassador Mohamed invited me to a coffee shop to meet with a couple of women from Somalia. Of course I accepted and set out with questions buzzing in my head. *What were they doing here?* Because Somalia is a lawless land, I knew they had no votes on the Commission floor. What could they want?

I arrived at the Palais's coffee shop and was introduced to two women dressed in their tribal clothes. I saw them look out with eager eyes and palpable anticipation, searching my face for answers—or maybe clues.

These women began, slowly and with caution, to share their stories. And as the thread of their tapestry began to unravel, I felt anger and disbelief stitch me up more tightly with every word they spoke.

They told me of how, five years earlier, most of the men in their village were killed by a volatile opposing tribe—brutally hacked apart with machetes and left for dead. All of the surviving women fled, desperately scrambling to find safety in the jungles and ditches and high tree branches around their village. Those who were discovered were terrorized, raped, and tortured.

The entire scene hauntingly reminded me of the harrowing news that drained out of Rwanda in 1994. And I was aghast that these women—these *human beings*—had to live through such hell while the rest of the world checked their BlackBerrys and waited for good parking spots at the mall.

Sickened through and through, I fought back tears as I listened.

The tension of these stories—or at least the tension that I felt—was most apparent in the accompanying sense of helplessness that set in. I cannot erase history. I cannot do away with memories. I cannot banish evil—as much as I'd love to.

When I shared my thoughts of relative ineptitude with the group, the women stared back at me . . . with gratitude. *"We just wanted someone from the U.S. to hear our stories."*

The next week I was set to deliver the U.N. Commission on the Integration of the Human Rights of Women and the Gender Perspective. And those women were on my mind. If there was nothing I could *physically* do for them—nothing I could provide for them materially—then I decided that a mention of their heartache and tribulation to the world audience would be the gift I could give them. However large or small it seemed, it was my gift. Incorporating their story into my speech gave them validation. It gave them a voice.

I don't care where you were born, or what what's in your bank account (if you have one). I don't think twice about the clothes on your back or what you may wear on your head. To me, the mere fact that *you are human* makes you valuable. That alone makes you precious.

Returning back home after that trip left me with several thoughts. First, at Longaberger, we strive every day to treat people with dignity: To see others as humans first, not just as customers or employees. We make it our goal to care deeply for the welfare of all those who trot the globe alongside us. After all, we're all on the same journey on this planet.

However, maintaining this mentality takes work. It's easy to get sidelined by personal goals and begin to view others' lives as a commodity to be traded or won. But if ever I feel the slow ebbing of this tide, I stop and I think about sitting in the coffee shop with Ambassador Mohamed and the Somali women. I remember each hard-earned line on each face, and I remember that *people are people.*

Who knows why we were born in America—why others have to worry about machete-wielding fanatics and we don't? Perhaps the important thing is not the question, or even the answer, but the mere act of *asking.* By simply asking the question, we open the door to empathy and understanding—which is the first step to sharing the heart of another.

So how are you doing with the asking? Are you open to pondering tough questions—or do you still find it easier to close your mind to the world? To slam the book shut and instead open your latest issue of *In Style?*

What do you do to stay grounded and show real love for others—especially those like the Somali women who don't have a voice of their own? Who in *your world* is straining to be heard? To be seen? *To be valued?*

How can you work to share your platform with them—to offer your voice if they have none?

Resolve to take small steps today. Start asking questions. And start sharing your voice.

Part 2
Integrity

7 The Legacy of Right and Wrong

Learning from Mom and Dad

I flew into the house in a burst of speed, screen door snapping shut behind me. Frantically pulling drawers open and half-slamming them in equal time, my 10-year-old hands rummaged through scant belongings to find the Scotch Tape, a needle and thread, and a roll of masking tape. Checking to see that no one had spotted my transgression, I turned on my heels, Keds nearly laying rubber on the kitchen linoleum.

My friend Danny was gone by now; he had run home to his yard of safety and intact tree branches, while I was pinned to the earth in my land of mistakes, working nervously to repair the damage before Dad returned home.

I didn't mean to do it, of course. I usually climbed the sturdy old pine in our backyard when I needed solitude. But this time, no thanks to the neighbor boys, I had made the unlucky decision to wiggle my way out onto the delicate maple behind the garage and next to our rabbit pen. And I guess that day I wiggled a tad too far, because before I could drop to my salvation, I heard the distinctive and unquestionable *snap* that comes when weight overtakes wood.

Branch still hanging askew despite its newly acquired bandage of tape and thread, my frenetic hands stopped repairing when I heard car tires chomping the gravel at the end of our driveway. I looked with disdain at my shoddy work and quickly ran away, removing myself from the scene of the crime.

The din of man and shoes came near and my body signaled the presence of another. Uh-oh.

"TAMI!! Come here. What did you do?" Dad barked.

"I didn't do it! Danny did it!" I lied.

"I see." He strode away without further comment, making a beeline for my helpless friend who most likely sat innocently eating his Swiss steak and mashed potatoes at their small kitchen table. Knocking on the front door, Dad asked to speak to Danny.

"Danny, can you tell me what happened to that little maple tree I have growing behind the garage?"

"I didn't do it!" he protested under the protective shelter of his own father. "Tami did it!"

"Oh. I see." With anger rumbling and eyes squinting with rage, he crossed back into our yard and found me cowering with guilt and remorse. He was *furious!* Speaking low and slow through gritted teeth, Dad let me know in no uncertain terms that lying would not be tolerated in the Longaberger household. I felt like a mere speck of humanity, embarrassed and drowning in guilt.

Dad grounded me for *three days*. It was the only time in my entire life I was grounded.

What I came to realize later was that once the lie escaped my lips, the condition of the Maple branch ceased to matter to my Dad. I got no credit for "trying to fix it." No amount of sewing and taping could "fix" the fact that I had been untruthful. I've never forgotten that lesson. The easy summary is—*don't lie!* But the more challenging lesson to digest is that sometimes words are irretrievable, and that, once lost, trustworthiness can be a difficult thing to patch up.

I've surmised over time that my position of CEO can prove thorny when issues of truth and falsehood are presented. Unfortunately, it seems some people are more concerned with pleasing me or preserving their image; so much so that, when retelling a story, they might *accidentally* leave out a few key pieces of information. These "partial truths" or incomplete disclosures become quite costly when used as the basis for weighty decisions. Because it is my job to place all considerations in the balance when resolutions need to be made, I have no choice but to move forward with the information placed in front of me.

Could the entire truth, if revealed, have produced a different outcome? Yes. Could the entire truth, if revealed, have swayed my decision? Changed my vote? Yes.

But when people run for masking tape and thread, I am left examining the branch for clues. And, after so many years in business, I have gotten *very good* at distinguishing honesty and trustworthiness. I know when to listen to my gut. I quietly discern the inflection of one's voice when sharing a story; watch to see if they fidget, shifting their eyes away from mine. Plainly put, *people who struggle to tell the truth will struggle with me.*

What my father taught me that day behind the garage was that character and integrity matter above all else—in business *and* in life. And even though nobody's perfect, if you live your life with integrity, you won't have to worry about "getting caught" or trying to hide something embarrassing.

Removing that kind of weight from your shoulders will help anyone stand taller—and whether you're swinging from trees or standing firmly with both feet on the ground, *that's a good thing.*

8 Right Is Right

Taking the High Road behind the Scenes

It's easy to claim to *have* integrity; however, it's far more difficult to shore up your integrity when there's a lot on the line. And like so many things in life, terrible circumstances can split your being into two hemispheres: that of emotion, and that of intellect.

Eric Bartow is a lovely young man who worked for us as an assistant golf pro at the Longaberger Golf Club in his early 30s. He's an athletic, blond-haired, blue-eyed father of a darling little boy; a great guy whose rapport with customers was fantastic, helping to garner the affections of legions of golfing guests. We love him and know that, while with us, Longaberger benefited from his hard work, cheerful attitude, and determination to put the customer first.

But like so many U.S. businesses in the economic downturn of those years, dipping revenues meant it was imperative for us to streamline our operations. We needed to trim down, and we knew it would be painful. In the offices and boardrooms of our corporate headquarters, decisions to slash operating expenses were being made, and sadly, Eric's position was on the list.

Knowing he had a wife and young child at home—and that he was truly an asset to the company—I didn't want to let him go. I hedged and procrastinated the inevitable for several reasons, not the least of which was that Eric had great customer service skills;

he was a valuable member of our extended family, making his release knotty and troublesome.

As fate would have it, while the termination list sat on my desk collecting dust, Eric was beginning a harrowing journey of another kind: He had been diagnosed with a brain tumor.

When news of Eric's condition reached me, I was stunned and heartbroken. Now what? I knew I couldn't keep him on the payroll, but I also knew I couldn't *NOT* keep him on the payroll. Losing his job would mean losing health insurance, and the results of such a move would be life threatening *at best.*

So instead of telling him anything about downsizing or terminations or layoffs, I talked to Eric about treatments and hospitals and specialists. I called doctors on his behalf, trying to get him into the best facilities as soon as possible. I made the decision to keep him on staff, despite a price tag of *up to a million dollars*—simply because I knew what *the alternative* would mean.

And how do you put a price tag on a human life? How could I possibly walk away from Eric, knowing that my good-bye would quite possibly be *good-bye?*

Eric endured the rigors of multiple surgeries and was shockingly reduced to a man I did not recognize for a small period of time during his treatment. I remember he called me on the way to the hospital for his first doctor's appointment, and he played his favorite song into the phone: *What a Wonderful World,* by Louis Armstrong. It struck me as a beautiful paradox: A man who was quite possibly dying was sharing his love for our world on his way to yet another round of tests and what-ifs. He could have chosen any number of songs recounting anger and injustice and melancholy. But instead, *wonderful.*

It gave me pause. It made me count my own blessings.

Wonderful, indeed. Wonderful to be in a position to make sure he had the health care he needed to live. Wonderful to play a part in keeping a father and a husband alive. Wonderful to give Eric another chance to sing. Eric gave me an opportunity to realize how very lucky I am—and I am grateful to him for that.

And five years later, Eric is still alive! He decided to leave the company some years ago on his own accord so that he could move to North Carolina to be near family. I rejoiced with him that he could enjoy life closer to those he loves, and I continue to cheer for him as he strives to rebuild a healthy, active life. As a celebration gift in honor of his bravery and will to overcome dire life circumstances, I even made arrangements to personally fly Eric and a friend to the Super Bowl in San Diego, California. He deserved a party!

Eric's story has a happy ending. Taking the high road, though costly, was an easy decision for me: Had I not done what I did, I couldn't have lived with myself. The emotional toll that it would have extracted to walk away from Eric and his health problems would have entirely snuffed out the joy I possess in my daily life. And nothing is worth the cost associated with a life full of regrets and despair.

Of course, there are decisions that prove much more precarious, and as CEO, I have to be willing to step forward and lead the way down a winding path of change. Even with the most astute counsel—the wisest people advising you—treading through a minefield of options can leave you shaken and second-guessing yourself.

It came to my attention some time ago that a friend of mine, someone with whom I attended high school, was struggling in her role as one of our Basketmakers. With her husband deployed in Iraq and no family to speak of, she was utterly stripped of a support system. An oppressive yoke of sadness throbbed against her skin and quickly became unshakable; she slipped into the abyss of depression. Crippled with grief and hopelessness, work became too much to undertake, and she stopped coming in for her shifts altogether.

We did all we could for her, and in our desperate desire to save her job, we *literally sent people to her home to drag her out of bed.* Yet she perpetually violated attendance policies. So we gave her another chance. And another. And another. And another. Trapped on the merry-go-round of history and emotion and logic, I fought against the inevitable.

And that's when it hit me: I realized that perhaps some people do have pure and perfect intentions. They mean to do well—to perform and excel. But despite all their if's and but's, they simply do not possess the skill set needed to complete the task. They just can't do it. And no amount of adjusting and accommodating will give you fruits and nuts—or a Merry Christmas. At that point, there aren't a lot of logical—or loving—options left.

I eventually had to let nature take its course and terminate my childhood friend. I had to say good-bye to the woman who had grown up next to me—who witnessed my transformation from grocery store clerk to business owner. And the worst thing about this decision was that I knew by firing her, I would lose her entirely.

Gone the Basketmaker.

Gone the friend.

Making these kinds of decisions imposes a heavy burden. It means walking a road fraught with tough choices and complex scenarios. But as with any integrity issue, your instinct and good will must be your guide. At Longaberger, I can only do my best, following my heart toward the ending that promises the greatest success for the majority of our family.

And so whether I'm doing it in the boardroom or the car, talking or texting on my cell phone, meeting face-to-face, clicking into a conference call, or clicking the channel on my TV, *integrity matters.* Whether it's in the spotlight or behind the scenes, I still know: *What's right is right.*

It's the only way for Longaberger to do business; and it's the only way for me to live.

9 Parenting with the End in Mind

How I Worked to Instill Responsibility and Work Ethic in My Children

Sitting with my assistant in the backseat of the car that was delivering me to a lunch appointment, my body jolted with the sharp twists and turns that seem to be an unavoidable hallmark of city driving. Lights blinked and flashed, horns blared, and the faint echo of sirens floated ghostlike through tinted windowpanes. Colors blurred together out of the corner of my eye as people hoofed the sidewalks of New York City—a giant smear of civilization evaporating before I could focus on any one single thing.

But then again, I wasn't *trying* to focus on any one single thing—except for the sound of the voice on the other end of the phone line.

I was talking to my daughter.

Claire is not the little girl she once was, or the one that so many people might remember her to be: a frolicking, pigtailed fourth-grader worried about nothing more than the latest animal she could rescue from the ditches of our nearby country roads. And though my heart pinches to remember the innocent days of mothering a nine-year-old—days filled with squeals and the delights of simple pleasures at home—I have never been prouder of who she is now: a wonderful college student with dreams in her head and feet on the ground.

Claire has grown into a lovely, well-rounded young woman with a good head on her shoulders and an even better heart beating within her. Like me, she loves nature, is gregarious and affable, and strives always to be her best. Like her brother, she diligently pursues her passions, is thoughtful, and realizes that the world will not be handing her anything on a silver platter. Instead, she knows that she'll have to work hard, prove herself, and grab for the brass ring just like we all do.

This particular phone call proved it: "Well, Mom," she ended, "I should probably go. I have to get to work."

My assistant, sitting to my left, heard the comment projected on speakerphone and sat at attention. Perhaps she was surprised that Claire would be a working college student? Perhaps she would be more surprised to discover that Claire works at *two* part-time jobs at Ohio State.

"You'd better! Girl, you need the money!" I said, spying a thinly veiled expression of shock on my assistant's face.

Growing up the way I did instilled in me the conviction that despite any circumstances, last names, or family legacies, kids have to be taught *how to work*. They must develop the character and resolve needed to make their own way in the world—to succeed and become self-sufficient.

As a parent, it's a hard balance to strike—one to which some of you reading this might be able to relate. You want so badly for your child to have the best, to not go without, to be *happy*. Yet you realize with maturity that happiness doesn't lie wrapped in shiny packages, no matter how pretty the bow.

At the same time—you recognize that childhood is fleeting, innocence is quickly lost, and friends, social events, and sports calendars begin to take over some of the real estate that only Mom and Dad once occupied. So how do you allow them to romp in the backyard, tear down the sidewalk on their bikes, chase after birds . . . and in the next breath, call them in for chores and teach them responsibility?

My own father was, of course, fiercely insistent upon my working through high school. And I'll be frank; he went overboard at times. Though he later admitted his error in judgment to me, it didn't erase the fact that I was denied the opportunity to attend my boyfriend's high school football games on occasional Friday nights—including the only time his rival school played ours. Instead, I was marooned inside Dad's store, stocking shelves! While I'm thankful that he apologized, it doesn't give me back those muggy July days and evenings that I longed to spend with friends, enjoying the last parcels of childhood being divided up by the remains of summer. It doesn't give me back nights of cheering at football games or laughing at school dances.

By the time I was a senior in high school, I had all of my credit requirements done and was able to leave the building at 11 AM It was a great concept—until my Dad realized what was happening. Upon hearing of my schedule, he took it upon himself to charter his own "vocational" school, if you will. I began leaving school early in the fall of my senior year to go work for him at the store three days a week—not including my weekend shift. Pricing food, stocking shelves, ringing up customers: all key ingredients in my final year at Tri Valley High School.

Despite the long shadow that my father casted—and still casts—I'd be remiss if I didn't mention the ways in which my

mother played a role in my perceptions of work. Being with Mom
was home for me, literally and figuratively. Rachel and I lived
exclusively with her growing up. We didn't shift back and forth
between her house and Dad's, we didn't negotiate weekend visits,
and we didn't fight over holidays. We lived with Mom—plain and
simple.

Perhaps more importantly to me at the time, it was home in
another sense, because it's where I felt the most myself—my true,
unedited self. My Mom was fantastic about encouraging me and
asking questions that helped me think. She let me spread myself
out, unfold my wings, and survey my options. Mom wanted me
to be *me*—and there's nothing more indicative of home than that.

If I'm being honest, I suppose I realized even then that living
with a single mother gives a person a new and different lens—
another way of looking at things. It dawned on me as a teen
learning about work and life without Dad present—except for in
small and unpredictable doses—that *my Mom needed to work*. It
was not a *choice* for her; there was no discussion or painful debate.
If we wanted food on the table, seeds for the garden, a roof over
our heads, gas in the car, and shoes for our feet, Mom had to
work.

In those years, my mother worked the swing shift—4 PM to
midnight—at the Good Samaritan Hospital in Zanesville, Ohio.
She went to great lengths to make sure that we were well taken
care of in her absence. She hired a woman named Twila Butler as
a housekeeper and nanny, so that Rachel and I wouldn't be alone.
We loved Twila and were grateful for her steady, tireless presence
in our midst. Because of her, I never came home to an empty
house the entire time I was growing up. She was with us until I
went off to college.

What I saw in my Mom then, and understand even better
now, is that her education, skill, and independence allowed her to

recover from a loveless relationship. She went back to college, earning her degree over the period of six years, graduating only slightly before I did, and doing so without fanfare or recognition. She knew that her hands would bring supper home and fill the gas tank. She knew that the sweat of her brow would purchase new shoes in the fall and small gifts at Christmas. If my mother had been uneducated and unskilled, what would have happened to our little family? I sometimes wonder.

It breaks my heart to see one human economically bound to another—shackled with the kind of chains birthed from a lack of choices. I've seen it happen too many times, and with dire consequences for all involved. So part of the reason that I wanted to teach responsibility and a work ethic to my children is because I would never want them to stay in a bad relationship with someone upon whom they had become financially dependent. I would never want them to sacrifice their dreams, their individuality, their emotional well-being, or worse—their personal safety—because they found themselves without a way to support themselves. People can't fly when they're backed into a corner.

One of the decisions that I made early on in my parenting was to make sure that my children had a frame of reference for the lives that they currently happen to enjoy. I tried to take vacations and do activities together that would expand their worldview. I helped them see that while Mom had a bank account, its contents weren't automatically and expressly passed on to them in the midst of their high school "emergency." I strived to teach them that work is a part of life—period. And theirs will be no different.

While we all have grand hopes for our futures, there are no guarantees in business or in life. I have told Claire and Matthew that life is uncertain, and that I won't always be there to pick them up—though I certainly would *like* to be! I want them to understand that eventually, they will need to pull strength and courage and purpose from the depths of their own souls without being able to call Mom for a hand up. And I have every confidence that my children have learned this.

The wise work, and the wise prepare. I'm trying my darndest to make sure they do both—and do both well.

Just like many of you, my rules spring from my deep love for each of them. Giving my kids the gift of a great work ethic and personal responsibility will serve them well—helping them navigate the rough waters of life and the uncertainty of our times. My hope is that Claire and Matthew will have learned how to balance life's expectations and duties with the kind of mental freedom one needs to *really dream*.

My kids are not carbon copies of me; I don't yearn for them to follow in my footsteps or insist that they make the same choices I made in work or education or social circles. I love them too much to chip away at their individuality and supplant them with idealistic, perfect little mimes.

But I do insist that they learn to work hard, to see the value in stretching their minds, to be deliberate about learning, and to remain, always, true to themselves.

And, of course, I hope they come out on the other end still—and always—loving their Mom.

10 Making Things Right

A Consultant's Story of Longaberger Values

One of the many luxuries Longaberger has enjoyed since our founding in 1973 is our customers' loyalty. Scores of stories have ascended to my seventh-story office about men and women who bought their first basket decades ago, only to shepherd their child into Longaberger as she grows and prepares to leave for college or establish her own home. It's a wonderful evolution, really: Mother sharing with daughter, passing on treasured heirlooms along with new pieces made for today's modern home.

It's not just the beauty and practicality of our baskets that foster allegiance and fidelity. Our customers also appreciate the craftsmanship displayed in our American-made ware. Like a growing number of citizens, these customers value quality products made *by hand* by *U.S. workers*. During these times of high technology and computers and mass production, *handmade* sets us apart and makes us unique.

Basketmaking has been in our family for over 100 years, handed down much in the same way that we expect our baskets to be. We use the same basic techniques today that my Grandfather J.W. knew so well and taught to his kids decades ago—the ones I have learned myself and that my own children have come to know. There's a history in what we do—a sense of legacy and Americana associated with Longaberger baskets that you won't find elsewhere.

Part of our success lies in the fact that we educate and instruct our Basketmakers on these techniques as they progress through a 20-week class on weaving. They learn to moisten the splints, weave a base, and manipulate our ergonomic equipment by raising or lowering the weaving horse to their comfort. They learn to position tiny nails, situate handles, fasten copper hinges, and sand down the edges. They learn to *care* about their craft because—like the work of a great artist—each basket is made by hand. It bears the initials of its maker and the year of its emergence from Longaberger.

Could our customers buy another basket at the local big-box store and pay less? Of course. Would it exhibit the personality— show the care and attention paid it by Americans who take pride in each of their works? Probably not. Those who truly view basketmaking as a nearly lost art come to value what millions of loyal customers already know: that "made in America" *matters*.

With such attention to detail, it's not surprising that we receive very few complaints or returns for quality reasons. Sure, there's the occasional basket that doesn't match someone's living room or doesn't neatly fit in the family room bookshelf, but in terms of *quality,* our numbers are outstanding. Still, our workers report to the plant each day with worries and preoccupations that get dragged along from their outside lives; and sometimes, despite all good intentions, those worries and preoccupations are woven into their craft. We cut and dye and weave a natural fiber with knots and natural grain variances; so just as no two days are alike, no two individuals are identical, no two pieces of wood are uniform—and no two baskets are absolutely indistinguishable. They are "perfect" in their very imperfections.

Yet invariably, problems do arise, and when they do, Longaberger goes out of its way to restore returned products to their once pristine condition—or find a way to rectify the situation.

Jeanné Wildman is a Branch Leader from California who has been with the company for nearly eight years. After hundreds of in-home parties and thousands of orders placed, Jeanné has had fewer than *10* returns for quality.

Recently, Jeanné shared with me that one of her customers—who we'll call "Pam"—had a cherished Cake Basket that was over 25 years old. The particular style of her basket had stationary handles, and after a quarter of a century of hauling birthday cakes and picnic goodies, one of the handles had broken off. Jeanné took the basket and promised to ship it back for a handle replacement—no questions asked.

The days grew long and soon Jeanné realized that one week—then two—had gone by—and still no word on the basket. Pam's daughter called Jeanné to check on the status of the repair, reminding her, "My Mom has never parted with that basket! It was a family gift and it means so much to her!" *No pressure,* Jeanné thought.

Not long after, Jeanné received a phone call from the company, hoping it would include the update she was looking for. However, the news coming her way was far from what she expected.

"I think we're walking into new territory here," said the voice on the other end of the line. "We got the shipping box and found a piece of paper inside, but we can't find a Cake Basket."

"What??" Jeanné was beginning to panic. It seemed that the shipping company had delivered an empty box! What would she tell Pam about the fate of her precious family heirloom?

"Yeah—there's no basket. If you want to talk to the customer and find out the exact year of the basket, we may be able to go into the archives of retired and treasured pieces and find a replacement—but even that isn't guaranteed. I'll have to talk to my supervisor."

Jeanné hung up, desperate not to have to reveal this awful turn of events to Pam. Although the missing basket was not her fault—or Longaberger's, for that matter—Pam had entrusted it to Jeanné, and she felt that the blame fell on her.

Gathering her courage, Jeanné took a deep breath and picked up the phone. With fingers crossed, she delicately explained the situation to Pam, laying out the options: Provide the year and hope for a miracle to emerge from the archives, or, she offered, accept a new version with swinging handles.

"Oh, my! Well, if I could get a brand-new one with swinging handles, I'd be just as happy!" Pam gushed.

Jeanné leaned against her kitchen wall, exhaling with relief that all was well in California—and exhaling doubly with a new respect for her company; one that works to make things right, even when empty boxes come into our returns center and we're left trusting in the good name of our consultants. We move forward in good faith because we value our customers and the reputation of the Longaberger name.

Baskets aren't the only thing that can wear over time, and while occurrences are exceedingly rare, our pottery can prove imperfect as well. Jeanné worked with another woman named Linda who had purchased our pottery *five years earlier,* and—although she loved it—she was beginning to notice some veining down the middle of one of her salad bowls. There were no cracks, no chips, but to the eye, it just didn't look "quite right."

"I can't guarantee anything at this point, Linda, since this bowl only carries a three-month guarantee, but let's send it in and see what happens." Carefully wrapping the piece in packing paper and bubble wrap, Jeanné boxed it up and sent it back to Dresden for inspection.

Luckily, since that particular salad bowl was still in production, Linda had a new bowl less than two weeks later. No questions asked. No hassle or fuss. Just making things right, one customer at a time.

At Longaberger, we believe in the small things. Gestures of appreciation doled out to customers who have remained faithful over years and decades. We believe in taking whatever steps may be necessary to revive an old basket or refresh a piece of damaged pottery. We know that we must take the high road and do whatever we need to in order to convey the powerful message of loyalty and integrity and sound reputation.

Several times a year, I get letters from people all over the country who have undergone a tragic life circumstance. These are often women who have been avid Longaberger customers, and who are reaching out after a personal hardship. They're searching for comfort and validation from a company they have grown to love, if even from a distance.

Just recently, I received one of these letters from someone named Marcy. Marcy explained that she had recently lost her home to a devastating fire. Everything was turned to ash—years of memories captured on film, family mementos, clothes, furniture, and *over 800 Longaberger Baskets.*

Yes—you read that correctly. *Eight hundred.*

Marcy wondered if I could do anything to help her begin her collection again. Perhaps a word of encouragement? A small gift? Anything?

My assistant brought me a Market Basket and a permanent marker so I could sign it before shipping it off to Marcy's new home. It is a ridiculously small drop in the bucket when you stop to consider the contents of a home: A lifetime of possessions and memories and history under one roof—up in smoke.

So for me to send Marcy a basket was just the right thing to do. I didn't provide her with a place to sleep, clothes for her back, or food for the pantry. It's not going to fuel her car or pay the bills.

But to Marcy, in that moment, it's a piece of the home she lost. It's a little bit of her past—her identity and her passion.

And for me, there's no question.

Whenever possible, we will go to great lengths to rise above the expected and the norm. We will do everything in our power to stand behind our products—whether they are 5 months, 5 years, or 25 years old.

Because anything less just wouldn't be right.

Anything less wouldn't be Longaberger.

Part 3
The Power of
Positive Thinking

11 "Getting It Right"

The Struggle toward Self-Confidence

When I take on a challenge, I give *everything I have* to make it a success. I pour every conceivable drop of energy and every pound of effort I can into a project, leaving myself thoroughly wrung out and exhausted because I *expect* to succeed. I would never begin something and think, *"You know—I'm going to shoot for 80 percent here."* That kind of thought process is utterly alien, completely foreign, and, frankly, absolutely unacceptable to me. When my name is attached to something, it is, in a most literal sense, a representation of *who I am*. And for that reason, I refuse to allow myself to be labeled *passable* or *all right* or *good enough* when it should be *great*.

Because I saddle myself with towering expectations—because I *expect to do well*—when I do succeed, I don't initiate raucous fanfare or wild applause. There's not a great deal to celebrate when *you expected the positive outcome in the first place*. I am pleased, of course, but I think, "Okay. That's what I was shooting for; now it's a reality, so on to the next thing." There isn't a surprise element or an unexpected twist at the end. It is what I was planning for, plain and simple.

The other side of the looking glass reveals an alternate reality dotted with disappointments and places where my arrow missed the target. Those are much more unsettling, of course, because they were wholly unwelcomed and not part of the plan. Receiving difficult news or sales figures levels me. It completely washes over any prize or achievement or accolade from yesterday. And for a time, it submerses my spirit.

When I stop to think about all the times in my life that I've come up short, the stack looms high and imposing—because *those* are the moments I remember. Though the world may see shine and polish and smiles, my memories are often disproportional to reality. Like a lunar eclipse blocking the gleam of midday sun, failures have a way of casting shadows and blotting out victories like ink spilling onto linen. I tend to dwell on the near misses, snags, and wrinkles in a garment that would otherwise spread silky and clean over the story of my life.

My dear friend Bernie Kosar can relate intimately to this kind of cerebral trip wire. Bernie played in the National Football League for 12 years as a quarterback with the Cleveland Browns, Dallas Cowboys, and Miami Dolphins. He still holds three NFL records and is widely regarded as one of the most beloved stars in Cleveland, where he spent most of his playing days and enjoyed tremendous success. But he doesn't remember the way he moved in the pocket or recall the litany of deftly thrown balls that led his teams to a win. He rarely looks back through time at a winning series he set into motion or the victories that felt so sweet. Instead, he ponders the disappointments—the critical fumble, the missed snap, the incomplete pass, the interception.

Although Bernie and I are optimists through and through, when it comes to evaluating *ourselves,* both of us tend to live in the shadow of an eclipse. We sit a little too long with our telescopes, staring at a round, buttery moon ensconced in the sun's path. And sometimes we lose sight of the big picture.

That's something we're both working on. We're trying harder to acknowledge the times we've gotten it right, drawing them out from the dark side of the moon so they can rightly bask in luminous sunlight. We're looking for times we can look back on and say, "Okay. I can be proud of *that.*"

When I take the time to seriously consider the things in life that I can be proud of—the things that have gone right and have helped underpin my self-confidence—three items stand out to me: my health, my newfound ability to say "no" in healthy ways, and my relationship with Bernie.

In the mid-1990s—although you'd never know it to look at him—my Dad was experiencing some heart trouble. Despite playing tennis three times a week and being thin and in shape, his arteries were struggling under the weight of plaque buildup and high cholesterol. Doctors informed him that if he didn't change his lifestyle and adopt a healthy diet, he would die of a heart attack.

I knew Dad was blindsided and confused. His regular meals of steak, mashed potatoes, and broccoli with cheese sauce seemed healthy enough for him, and to be honest, I wasn't a whole lot more educated than he was at the time. What would a healthy diet look like? What would it mean for his lifestyle? I knew that since Dad wasn't married, tending to these adaptations rested on me, and that meant I had to get started reading, investigating, and researching.

Sitting with my father at the out-of-state specialist's office was not only a wake-up call for him; it was an unexpected blessing and unforeseen wake-up call for me. Dad's efforts to save his own life ended up *preserving my own.*

I began to think more critically about what I ate. I got more serious about working out. I started to see the connection between my health and the future I wanted to have with my children, the future of my role at Longaberger, the future I wanted to spend full of joy, with freedom and mobility. I knew it was up to me. I knew I had to take the reins—and I did.

Even now, more than a decade later, fitness is paramount to my outlook on life and my emotional well-being. I've learned to channel my energy in the weight room or yoga studio. When I have a particularly stressful day or feel overwhelmed by the demands of life, I know that I need to get outside and take a walk, or hop on the treadmill and sweat it out. It has become a companion that secures my feet to the ground, maintaining my balance and positive outlook.

Striving for health has bolstered my self-confidence, and it's one thing that brings me great pride. You only get one body and one lifetime to care for it. Neglecting your health is a costly gamble, and one I'm not willing to take. So, thank you, Dad! Your heart scare catapulted my campaign to be as healthy as I can be, and at last I'm able to say, "I got it right."

Taking the time to exercise and stay healthy meant revamping my overworked schedule and making some changes that at times were admittedly inconvenient. It meant that there were things I would have to remove from my schedule in order to accommodate an hour in the gym every day. It meant that I had to learn to be selfish about my time—in a good way. In short, I had to learn to say "no."

Saying no is tricky for many people—and, I believe, for women in particular. We're fixers. We want to be helpful. We don't want to offend anyone. We feel guilty if we say no and are terrified that we'll be perceived as self-centered—*especially* if there's no *"good reason"* to decline an invitation or request. It's a terrible hamster wheel of emotion that goads us into continually committing to things we're either not capable of or not prepared to complete. In truth, saying yes to avoid all of these negative feelings means we're really not saying yes to the invitation or request—we're saying yes to our ego. We're obliging merely to avoid social rejection, judgment, or the disappointment of another.

Is that a good reason to say yes? Would your friend really appreciate your presence at her event if she knew you didn't *want* to be there, but that you did it only because you didn't have a good enough excuse to skip it?

We need to rethink our definitions of kindness and selfishness. Is it selfish for me to spend an hour exercising? It is selfish to strive to remain healthy and live a long life with those I love? Of course not! Is it not infinitely more selfish to gorge myself on cheeseburgers and French fries and milk shakes, jeopardizing my heart health and potentially leaving my children without a mother—leaving any future grandchildren without the knowledge of their grandmother?

What I've come to realize about saying "no" is that it is *my choice;* and it is *your choice.* There are a finite number of hours in the day, and how we parcel them out is up to each of us. When I commit to something, I intend to be fully present, fully engaged, fully *there*. If I don't think I can do that, I will not make the commitment. Not only is it unfair to me and to my time, it's unfair to the person on the other end of the commitment. I owe that person my best and to be mentally and emotionally in the moment. If I can't, I shouldn't be there.

In years past, I felt like I had to be everything to everyone. Maybe some of you can relate to that feeling. I felt like I had to take on duties and responsibilities and tasks, and do every single one of them *well*. I felt like I just couldn't say no and let someone down. But strangely, I began to see that in doing so, I was letting *myself* down. In instances where I really didn't want to be there or do that, I began to resent the person who asked me. I began to seethe in quiet anger. Bitterness soured my tongue as I contemplated the hours of lost time and energy.

How ridiculous, of course; I had no right to be upset when *it was me who said yes!* If I didn't truly, authentically want to participate, I should have politely declined. My resentment was no one's fault but my own. The trouble with me—and so many others—is that we like to help. I'd help everyone if I could. But I *just can't.*

If you're someone who struggles with saying no, *even when you know you should,* ask yourself: Is it a true kindness—a sincere gesture—to commit to something with reservations and resentment hanging over you? What things are you doing right now that, rather than giving you energy, steal your joy? *You owe it to yourself to step back.* If you can't do something wholeheartedly, *you owe it to yourself to get out. Protect your time, your heart, and your joy.*

Make your "yes" yes, and your "no" no. Period. Because at the end of the day, you'll be judged on the things you say "no" to—not on the things you say "yes" to.

Choose wisely.

Decluttering my life made it easy for me to choose wisely when I met Bernie. My physical health, emotional well-being, and spiritual life were beginning to align, and I was finally learning to listen to my instincts in a way that I hadn't for years.

Bernie and I met each other through a mutual friend, and it was just the right time in our lives for things to work. If it had happened any earlier, I doubt it would have been as ideal for either of us. We wouldn't have been ready for each other in the way that we are now. There were things we had to endure, things we had to learn, and things we had to overcome to get to where we are today. I am not the same woman I was 20 years ago—or even 5 years ago. I am older, more mature, and I know what I can handle, what I want.

Coming to accept this change in my humanity and personality was an interesting shift for me. I used to cling to the idea that relationships were eternal. A friend was a friend forever. A spouse would always be in your life. Your children would always need you in the same way. And that employee would stay with the same company for decades.

But now I can see that this simply isn't true for everyone in every circumstance. There are times when it's okay to turn the page—when letting nature run its course is the best possible option. And sometimes it's not easy, but you have to believe that when one door closes, another will open.

And God opened a door for me with Bernie. After my painful and life-changing divorce, the loss of my Dad, and my struggle through many difficult years of transition and learning, Bernie came into my life at just the right time. And for that I'm grateful.

There's an old saying that goes like this: "People come into your life for a reason, a season, or a lifetime."

It hasn't been easy to meet someone who organically understands my life. Because—let's be honest—being in a relationship with a recognizable persona is not *normal*. It isn't *normal* to have your meal interrupted so that you can sign an autograph or snap a picture. It still doesn't feel completely *normal* for women to run up to Bernie, pawing and gushing while he makes their acquaintance. *But that's our life.*

Recently, in fact, we were in New York City at St. Patrick's Cathedral. Ancient columns stretched upward in the dimly lit sanctuary, stained glass windows gleamed like photos in a family album, staring through time and history. With shoes clicking down the tiled floor, we snuck into the rear chapel, a small, private place of worship and solitude; a place where no pictures are allowed and few even enter.

Both of us grew still, taking in the sacred space around us, feeling the mysterious weight of something bigger, something more wonderful than eyes can see. And we began to pray. To think. To consider our lives and our place in this world. It was a significant moment for us both: To stand there and just *be*. With each other. With God. With whispers in our hearts.

Then, suddenly, thunderous footsteps closed in and the heavy wooden door clanged open behind us, slicing our holy silence; veils of prayer and communion fell to the floor in a heap of abrupt interruption.

"Oh, my goodness! YOU'RE BERNIE KOSAR!" the voice bellowed into the smallness. "Oh, my word—I *love* you! I loved watching you play for the Browns! You were the *BEST!*"

"Thank you," Bernie replied in a quiet, humble voice.

"I just can't believe it's you—here at St. Pat's! WOW! I didn't even know you were Catholic! It's just so great to meet you!" The man rambled on, oozing compliments and rhapsodizing his status as super-fan.

I felt the familiar squeeze of Bernie's hand in mine, signaling his efforts to be patient and kind and gracious in the most inappropriate and private of times. I squeezed back, my way of saying, *"I get it. I know. I understand."*

Believe it or not, it's difficult to find someone who can relate to the kind of bizarre reality we live in. It's even more difficult to find someone who not only *relates* but doesn't let it affect them *or the relationship.*

Being with Bernie means being with someone who "gets me." He knows that I so appreciate our customers and collectors that he'll gladly join me in signing baskets; or he'll happily step aside while I do my job. He doesn't pine for the spotlight. He doesn't need propping up or constant reassurance. My success is not threatening to him. He loves me and supports me for who I am— not for where I work or whose daughter I happen to be.

So, for this—and for a million other small reasons—he's a "lifetime" kind of person. I appreciate his risk-taking personality, how he can still roll with the punches and get back up when he's knocked down. I value his ability to think on a macro level. I'm thankful for his business sense and his energizing personality. He has four beautiful children and understands how to walk the line with past marriages and relationships. He supports me and doesn't clamor for first place. He knows who he is and he knows who I am, and together we'll figure out where we're going. Together, we'll get it right.

And in my world, that is truly priceless.

12 Our Minds Are Double-Edged Swords

The Power of Positive and Negative Thinking

If I had to state a philosophy on life—a motto for living, so to speak—it would be that *life is a journey.*

It has taken me a while to learn that and then to really *believe it;* but over time, I truly have. And now I'm living it.

It can be so easy when we're young to become sidelined by the pit stops instead of seeing the big picture. So easy to become distracted by the supposed *destinations* of an imagined future: "When I graduate from high school, life will *really* begin. I'll be out of my parents' house and on my own! No curfews, no detentions—only freedom!" *And then* . . . "I can't wait to graduate from college and start a real job. I'll be able to get out of this campus housing and get my own place and shop at Ikea. I'll throw dinner parties and get pretty shoes and buy a briefcase. It'll be awesome." *And then* . . . "I can't wait until I meet someone and settle down. We'll take glamorous vacations to Bali and order fruity drinks with miniature umbrellas delivered to our lounge chair by a bellboy wearing white shorts. We'll sleep in on Saturday and read the paper on Sunday and it will be *perfect*."

Have you been there? Have you succumbed to this kind of thinking? The danger in putting your faith in "destinations" rather than the *journey* is that you're always looking over the next hill—always scanning the horizon for something different and better and more exciting. And in doing so, you miss the landscape streaming past your window. You miss the beauty and the precise nature of that moment in time. When you fail to see the joy in small things, you miss the joy of life! Because life is a lovely amalgamation of small moments that combine to form your story.

Remaining positive for me means finding value and hope and appreciation in the small things. I don't wait or bottle up my celebration for the really "big" moments. I don't hold tight to my laughter, "saving it up" for something outrageously funny. I don't stuff my joy, waiting for colossal events like weddings and babies and extra zeroes in my bank account. I let it flow freely each day in mundane, pedestrian moments that seem vanilla and ordinary. Because *those* moments make up life.

I make choices in the hours and minutes of my life. If I'm driving down a highway tangled with cement and abandoned buildings, trash skipping through ditches and over medians, I'll purposely fix my gaze on the trees. I'll center myself on the clouds, floating above like floured masses of bread dough on an azure kneading board. I'll watch the trees swaying in the wind. I'll find the beauty that I know is there—*somewhere*.

Searching for beauty and making it a choice from minute to minute accumulates to form a positive mind. Just as saying no to a pile of potato chips at lunch each day will add up and produce positive, healthy results, making small mental adjustments will do the same. Positive people don't exude positivity accidentally. They purposefully search for the opportunities to find the positive in daily choices—so a summation of those daily thought processes over time morphs them into someone with a sunny disposition. It takes practice and resolute thinking and acting, repeated over and over until it simply becomes *you*.

I used to find that making small mental adjustments toward the positive was a bit more challenging. Years ago, when my children were little, I remember racing out the door like a lunatic, grabbing a cup of coffee in a frenzy, trying not to let it slosh all over my freshly dry-cleaned suit. Yelling at the kids to find their shoes and haul their backpacks out to the car, I would steal a glimpse of my watch and feel my blood pressure spike as the minutes ticked away.

One morning I flung my briefcase on top of the car as I sped to secure the kids' seatbelts. I threw the car into reverse and careened out of the driveway on our way to day care, only to glance in the rearview mirror and witness a torrent of papers flapping from my briefcase and into the wind. Mercy! I couldn't even think straight enough to make sure my belongings made it into the vehicle!

Finding the positive when my work was strewn up and down the rural roads of Ohio was straining, to say the least. But when I caught a minute of quiet—in the elevator on my way up to my office, perhaps, or in a bathroom stall—I would pause and breathe deeply. I would stop to consider my blessings. *I had two beautiful, healthy children. I had a home and a reliable vehicle. I still had a briefcase—albeit an empty one! I had a job I loved and people around me to support me. I would be okay. Life was still okay.*

I'm no longer running out the door with toddlers in tow, but I am facing a new set of trials and tests. Our economy has changed drastically. People value different things than they used to; their shopping habits have changed. Our nation is at war. The climate of the world is a shifting, dynamic, unpredictable creature. And businesses are floating in the midst of that swirling, tumultuous expanse.

So if I know that I have a particularly demanding day ahead of me, perhaps packed with meetings and tense discussions, I will get up a little earlier than normal. I will take 20 minutes to sit outside and watch the fog lift from the surface of my pond or take a walk in the backyard. I will breathe in the air and the dew and the mist of morning. I need that solitude—that moment of silence and stillness to calm my soul.

I make the choice to feed my spirit at the start of my day, to surround myself with things I love and find beautiful. To allow myself to wake up next to ducks and birds and squirrels rather than the loud hum of copy machines and the peal of telephones ringing.

Interestingly, I also believe that you need the counterbalance of sadness to really feel the joy that comes with positive thinking. Would I enjoy the lovely dance of native Ohio prairies or the statuesque oaks rising from the grove floor if I didn't know the ugly reality of nature abused? Would it mean as much—or be as precious to me—if I'd never seen a once-picturesque lake filled with old tires and noxious trash?

I believe that the heights of joy and celebration and love can only truly be known after the valleys of despair and disappointment have also been traversed.

When I was going through my divorce, days grew dark and lonely, and I threw everything into question—tossed it all to the wind. I second-guessed myself; I felt worry and guilt nag at me, tugging on my sleeve like a lost child. I made bad choices; I didn't take care of myself; I grew complacent and angry. I wasted time going places and seeing people just to fill the evenings. The weight of the sky seemed to drop lower and lower, clouds converging overhead.

I'd be lying if I said it was still easy to remain positive. The truth is that it was profoundly burdensome. I had to make deliberate choices every hour of every day. I had to *choose* to look for the light among the shadows.

My father's death came within weeks of the divorce and rubbed more grainy salt in fresh wounds. I had lost my Dad—my guiding light and confidant. I had left an unhealthy relationship and faced returning to a cold, empty home, alone. I was miserable, and my trust had been shattered.

Sorrow pulled on my ankles like a millstone, feet slipping with each unsteady step. I knew I could not let myself sink. I reached out for the few friends I knew were still trustworthy and fully available to me. They helped shore up my wilting joy, reinstate a measure of faith in humanity, and buoy my spirit. I am so grateful to each of them for their love and the grace they imparted.

Having been at the heights, floating through starry heavens on carpets of great success, I can tell you that those moments are all the sweeter after having known the deep pit of sadness and regret. To fully appreciate one, you must know the other. And so both positive *and* negative thinking prove powerful. Both are necessary to expand your emotional range. Both are necessary to fully appreciate the gifts and blessings and hardships that come our way.

To revel in pleasure, you must first know pain.

To climb high, you must first be brought to your knees.

To squeal with delight, you must first know searing sadness.

Life can sometimes feel like a battle, but it's all about perspective. And it's all about the choices you make daily and hourly that will inform how you'll wield your double-edged sword.

So—do you need to choose to wield your sword in a more positive way? Do you find that you often fall into the trappings of negativity? Are you being suffocated by joyless people who cause you to ferment and wither?

Can you identify a moment of profound joy—or sadness—that has since informed your life by allowing you to more fully appreciate successive highs and lows? Have you allowed your thinking to be changed by that moment or encounter?

Remember, life's a journey made up of small moments and split-second decisions. Choices that may at first glance seem inconsequential and unimportant pile up and become *a life*.

Choose to make yours great.

13 Finding Balance

A Four-Part Recipe to Positive Thinking and Harmony

Corporate decisions can be excruciating to make and emotionally draining to execute. If you let them, petty disputes and daily nuisances will buzz around your head, grating on your nerves and leaving you raw, unable to scratch the itch that keeps you up at night. A demanding family life, a busy calendar, and lack of time to recharge all combine to spell disaster if you don't purposefully maintain a healthy, balanced life.

Without the power of positive thinking, it would be much more challenging to find the joy of work *or* the love of life. But over time, I've learned how to live in the moment, walk through this journey, remain focused on the positive, and maintain balance in a shifting world. And in doing so, I've pieced together a litany of beautiful moments that, when amassed together, produce a masterpiece. Sometimes I just have to take a step back to absorb it; to more fully appreciate the artwork emerging from a life lived to the fullest. It's in those moments of distance and removal that I remember what a joy it is to be alive.

I brim with gratitude that I was born—that my mother brought me into this world kicking and screaming and announcing my existence to the autumn-colored planet. I am filled with thanks to be alive.

I am glad to go to work; to be of sound mind and healthy body and *able* to do my job.

I am glad for the dreams of my father. For risks taken and responsibilities assumed. For baskets and weavers and humble beginnings.

I treasure the choices available to us in this country. Americans can choose what to do, where to go, what to believe or dismiss, and *how to think*. And truly, being happy or sad is *our* choice to make.

As I assess my own mental and emotional standing, I know that there is more to consider than just what's happening at the office or in the kitchen or living room of my home. After years of experience, years of life, and years of mistakes, I have learned that to be complete—to be balanced and whole—you must set aside time to examine all aspects of your world: your work life, your personal life, your family life, and your spiritual life.

When I talk about your "personal life," I'm talking about *your relationship with yourself*; how you view *you* as a person. Are you spending time alone? (Brushing your teeth doesn't count!) Do you ever wrestle with thoughts and dreams, aspirations and regrets? Do you give yourself enough room to breathe, enough space to consider the trajectory of your fledgling life? Or do you cram your days so full that your mind never stops spinning long enough to land on the topic of *you?*

Taking that kind of time has become paramount to me. Enjoying a walk on the beach or a stroll through the meadows gives me time to reflect, reassess, recharge, and regain my footing. Spending 25 minutes outside, to breathe in the air, to ride my bike, to see life unfolding before my very eyes—nothing is so peaceful as that.

I used to feel guilty about those walks. I would waste those precious minutes worrying that I was inconveniencing someone else or missing out on something happening elsewhere. I tripped through messy thoughts, nearly frantic that I should be returning that phone call or replying to her e-mail—as though 25 minutes were a lifetime and a sacrifice of giant proportion!

Now, with age and experience, I acknowledge that denying myself a small, airy cushion of peace and solitude only leads to a flattened spirit. Eyes blink lifeless and fatigued. I become an empty shell, a hollowed-out member of humanity longing for meaning and direction.

Ignoring my personal life leads to ruin and empties me in an awful way. In the same manner, neglecting my family life and denying their love leaves me unmoored in an ocean of loneliness. Forsaking my spiritual life leads me down a path of searching and longing for something bigger than myself. And abandoning my work denies me valuable creative outlets. It denies me the opportunity to contribute to something that will outlast Tami Longaberger.

We need all four of these parts, and they each require constant adjustments, frequent alterations, and perpetual accommodations. We must resolve to take stock of each one, each day.

Imagine a meter, similar to the gas gauge in your vehicle, keeping track of the overall health and "fullness" of your personal, work, family, and spiritual lives.

How full are yours right now? What areas are running on "low"?

Are you overindulging one of the four at the expense of the others? Why is it difficult to say no—*or not now*—to that component? How is your family being affected by your choices? Do you believe you're heading in the right direction?

If you need help deciding how to portion your time and energy, ask yourself, "When I'm 80 years old, what will matter about this decision?" Stopping to ponder this, if only for a few minutes, offers needed perspective to the thickness.

And while taking a moment to eat an apple on the front porch may not seem important to tomorrow or next week or when you're 80, remember: *It's a journey*. Allowing yourself small moments to exhale and decompress *will matter tomorrow*.

So unfold your legs and arms and let your mind stretch. Give yourself permission to live in harmony.

Part 4
Enthusiasm

14 Reflecting on a Legacy

Dad's Enthusiasm Was Contagious

Leaning back against the noisy vinyl of the booth, I stretched my legs under the linoleum-clad table and waited for my Dad. Meeting at either the Windemere or the Market House in Zanesville on Fridays after work was quickly becoming our tradition. Sometimes other staff members would join us and Dad would buy a round. Other times, it was just him and me sipping away our cares together.

That night, my Dad blew in through the door and found me by the window nursing a glass of red wine. He located our server and ordered his standard Crown Royal and Coke. Plasticky seats gave way as he bounced over to a comfortable position, exhaling loudly and smiling broadly.

"What a week, huh?" he said, clapping his hands together with a happy mix of relief and excitement.

It was the mid-1980s, and Dad and I were trying valiantly to work out our personal relationship *and* keep the business afloat. We had bills to pay, and we were not yet profitable. We couldn't figure out how to keep all the balls in the air; it left us trying desperately to master a delicate juggling act while maintaining

cool veneers of reassurance and confidence. We nearly went
bankrupt more than once during those years. It was a very taxing,
demanding time that exacted an emotional and mental toll on
us all.

Dad and I bantered and ate dinner, laughing and reliving the
crazy moments of Tuesday and Wednesday and Thursday. We
rehashed the events of Friday and talked about the next days and
weeks ahead.

But really, all I could think about was how eternally *glad* I was
that it was the weekend! I couldn't wait to go out with my
girlfriends after we left the restaurant. I couldn't wait to sleep in
and spend Saturday doing absolutely *nothing*. I wanted a break—
wanted some time to think about anything but baskets.

Scraping my plate with the side of my fork and wiping my
mouth clean, I drank the last of my wine and pulled on my coat.
And that's when I looked up and saw Dad looking at me with eyes
sparkling.

"Well, I gotta get home and get to bed," he said! "I got a lot
of things to do tomorrow! Tami, *I can't wait to jump out of bed in
the morning!* It's another day—another fresh start."

I stared at him, the beginnings of a smile starting to push
on my cheeks. I loved that man. I loved that he could plow
through difficulty and come through smiling, beckoning forth
another day.

He was so excited about his new ideas and thoughts on the
future of Longaberger. His enthusiasm and determination were
positively contagious, surrounding him like some kind of rare
angelic halo. It wasn't his education or his resources that set him
apart and made him special. It was his enthusiasm.

I'll never forget when the governor of Ohio came to Dresden
to talk about the existing jobs in manufacturing. With speech

prepared and talking points in line, all Dad could do was bend his ear with a plethora of tourism ideas. He raved about his vision for creating a corporate headquarters in the shape of a basket. He waxed on about building a "Longaberger Homestead" that would combine retail shopping and dining opportunities.

The governor stared at him, nodding politely. I like to think that he could see the halo of Dad's glow, too. He could see the enthusiasm that spilled over, pooling at Dad's feet and splashing his ankles.

That memory encapsulates my father perfectly. If you gave him the chance to talk, he'd take it and run, begging to tell you about how great life was, how fantastic the company was, and how it would be even better in the future.

Dad's enthusiasm continues to shape me—and, by extension, our entire company. We still glean joy and laughter from his memory. We still remember his energy, his positivity, and his will to succeed.

And because of him, I can now say with honesty that I can't wait to get out of bed in the morning, grateful for another day and a fresh start.

15 From the Homestead to the Office

Promoting Enthusiasm

Sometimes life orchestrates a seemingly fateful intersection with individuals whose enthusiasm can nearly blind us to the realities of their lives. Sometimes their gleaming smiles fool us, leaving us to wonder if their enthusiasm emanates from a carefully suspended mask—or if it truly radiates from a heart overflowing.

When I met Kelli McVay several years ago, I was not fooled. I knew without a doubt that her enthusiasm—that magical, sparkling "something"—was indeed an authentic outpouring of joy.

I would come to find out later that Kelli was a single mother of two struggling to free herself from the trappings of an unsafe relationship. While juggling tedious divorce proceedings and the never-ending demands of motherhood, Kelli was also taking college classes. Determined to complete her teaching degree, she was modeling strength and perseverance to her children. And as if that wasn't enough, she worked part-time with Longaberger in our Entertainment and Events Department at the Homestead.

Charged with choreographing dancers, hiring freeze models for the sidewalks, and managing entertainers, Kelli was also chiefly responsible for creating and executing all shows at the Homestead. Drawing on her past experience teaching dance classes, Kelli threw herself into her work, loving every moment. But what she loved even more was encouraging and supporting her team members— one of whom was my daughter, high school sophomore Claire Kaido.

When Kelli recalls the summers that Claire spent working as a singer in the Entertainment troupe at the Homestead, she notes how personable and open she was. She told me that Claire conducted herself with such poise, suggesting that so many other 16-year-olds in her shoes might work with an air of superiority or waltz in expecting special treatment. According to Kelli, Claire was just the opposite: Punctual, kind, mindful of the rules, polite. As her mother, I couldn't have been prouder of this report.

Although Claire began at the Homestead with considerable choir participation, she had little experience as a solo singer at that time. Kelli recalled her as being open and teachable, willing to receive guidance and constructive criticism with grace.

I watched Claire on stage from afar, wanting her to have her own identity and time to shine. From my vantage point behind the crowd, I noted Claire's joy behind the microphone but also witnessed the care and attention that Kelli paid to every entertainer. She exuded positivity, inspiration, and motivation, and Claire responded to her with ease and gladness. It was then that I first noticed Kelli's gift for teaching and encouraging.

After a series of events a few summers ago, Kelli sent me a kind e-mail thanking me for the support that Longaberger had extended to her during those difficult years of trial and adjustment. She was so grateful for the flexibility we extended to her while she scheduled her college classes and worked to raise two children as a single mother in the midst of it all.

Kelli's e-mail shared how in those days, being newly divorced and alone, *Longaberger was her family*. We gave her opportunities to work and succeed despite difficult circumstances at home. She learned how to balance work and school and mothering. Kelli felt indebted to us, when the case truly was that *we* were indebted to *her* for her undaunted display of enthusiasm.

Opening that e-mail confirmed my notion that Kelli had so much more to give, so much more to offer than what dance shows required. Kelli's big smile deserved a big arena, and I decided to offer it to her in the form of a new job: Sales Development Manager at the Big Basket.

I picked up the phone just as the 2008 holiday season began to chime. "Kelli, hi! It's Tami Longaberger. How are you?"

The surprise and delight on the other end of the line was unmistakable, making the purpose of my call that much more exciting. I went on to explain that I could see Kelli was passionate about teaching and encouraging others, and that it was obvious that she gave her all to whatever she undertook. I told her that if she was interested and willing, we could certainly use her enthusiasm to help train and guide our national sales force.

"Does that sound like something you'd like to do, Kelli?" I asked hopefully.

I assumed that the silence on the other end meant she was either dancing happily around the kitchen, weighing her options, or trying to figure out a way to politely decline.

"Tami, I am so honored. I would *love* to come to work for you at the Corporate office. But I have to tell you, I've been going to college for *seven years,* taking one class at a time, finagling them in between day care and work and a thousand other things. My kids have seen me turn my world upside down to get this education, and I still have to do my student teaching this January and February. There's nothing I would love more than to take the job, but I just can't give up my dream of graduating. And more importantly, I can't send that message to my children—especially to my daughter."

I listened with pride as she filled in the gaps in her story and shared her heart with me. Kelli's little girl, Kenzie—then just six years old—had been witnessing her mother's strength. She saw her mom work tirelessly on homework and projects. She saw firsthand the sheer exhaustion and dogged determination, and understood that her mother was doing this for her good and the good of her older brother, Cameron. She saw her mother model commitment so that they could live freely and without worry.

Above anything else, Kelli wanted both of her children—but especially her daughter—to learn that women can respect themselves, pull themselves up and out of bad situations, and live a life worthy of applause and celebration.

"So, Tami," she continued tentatively, "would it be alright if I complete my student teaching and then come and work for you in March?"

"Of course!" I nearly yelled into the phone. "I can't think of a more honorable, wonderful thing for you to do. You go get that degree. You show your kids what commitment looks like. I'll be right here cheering for you—and the job will be waiting."

Kelli has continued her career climb to this day. She's now working as Field Development Manager, training and mentoring our entire sales force in the southern part of the United States. Working side by side with sales leaders, she takes time to explain Longaberger's career plan, helping to guide those who come to her with new goals and aspirations. Kelli draws upon her education degree each day that she coaches a new consultant or sits down to teach someone new techniques to grow their business. And just as a teacher encourages and rejoices in the success of a student, so does Kelli.

The enthusiasm that caught my eye at the Homestead is now shining brightly here at the Big Basket. It gives me great joy to see that Kelli is not only working to her fullest potential, but that she was able to rise above her circumstances and continue to radiate her brilliant, contagious, inspiring enthusiasm.

And it pleased me even more that, in the midst of it all, her children could see her determination. That her son could learn from her tenacity and resilience; that her daughter could behold such steadfast commitment to dreams and finishing what was started. That she would believe that circumstances, past or present, did not *define* her mother.

And now—for the yet unnamed baby girl waiting to burst into our world this summer—that she will grow up hearing the stories of her mother's strength. She will grow up hearing of her mother's fortitude and virtue.

Life certainly orchestrated something beautiful when it composed the soundtrack of Kelli's life. We're all listening—and we're all applauding.

16 Feeding Joy

How I Remain Enthusiastic

October wind whips and swirls, tickling the leaves on so many towering trees outside my kitchen window. They flash crimson and persimmon and goldenrod. They are flat and crunchy and *lovely*.

I adore autumn not only because of the wonderful displays of creativity going on in the world around us, delirious splashes of color boasting beauty in the sunlight of afternoon. I love autumn because of what this season means: fresh apples sliced and sprinkled with cinnamon and nutmeg, folded safely into a flaky pie crust, the heavenly smell baking into every corner of my home. Flaming pumpkins and gourds that remind me of Grandma's garden, of hollowing out birdhouses from dried vegetable carcasses—new tombs that spring life for birds.

I love the return of canary-yellow school buses to our country roads. Even though my children have graduated from these giant taxis, their reappearance springs hope in my mind of children learning, making friends, and beginning on their paths into brilliant futures.

And of course, for our family, fall means football. The deafening roar of the crowd echoing off the field, the smell of grass and sweat and popcorn, the bright flicker of possibilities when a team of young men bursts into the stadium, galloping across yard lines and zigzagging onto the turf.

If there is ever a time for wild, boisterous enthusiasm, it is during a football game. I clap and scream and stomp my feet and shake my fists in the air. I don't care who sees me or what my hair looks like when I'm jumping up and down. I throw myself into the moment with passion and abandon. Being in the stadium with thousands of other crazed and jubilant fans energizes me in a way that few other things do.

But enthusiasm in other cities and states and buildings doesn't always look like it does in a football stadium. It can be a difficult thing to pinpoint, especially in a boardroom or office. When I'm at work, I may not jump and stomp like I do at games, but my heart leaps with an equally vibrant, intellectual enthusiasm when I think about our company.

For me, this kind of enthusiasm is more of the quiet joy that I find in learning and sharing moments with my children. It's about opening my mind, making new discoveries, asking hard questions. *That* makes me excited, gives me enthusiasm for each day, and prompts me to look forward to tomorrow.

Many years ago, I served on a board with a man who was highly respected in the business and marketing worlds. The list of companies he has founded and goals he has achieved is long and impressive. So one day, I said to him, "How do you do it? How do you personally keep pace with the growth of your companies?"

He told me, "Tami, be deliberate about learning. As the owner of your own company, no one's going to push you to grow. It's going to be up to you."

That singular comment flipped a switch in my brain that has spurred me on ever since. I became fervent in continuing to explore and expand my knowledge base. If I want to stay ahead of the curve and remain current and knowledgeable—it's completely *up to me.*

The kind of power that I possess to direct my future gives me enormous enthusiasm and drive. I want to be the kind of leader, person, and parent who is informed and well read. I want to wake up each morning excited to usher in more years of discovery. What a great approach to life!

As you can probably imagine, my zeal for learning has rubbed off on my children in some unexpected ways. For example, Matt and I were laughing about one of our early trips to Yellowstone. He was all of seven years old, and Claire was probably nine. We were staying at the Old Faithful Inn in the heart of our nation's oldest national park.

Dawn broke with July sun prying through the mist. Inside, our family was making a halfhearted attempt at getting ready for a day outside. The kids moved slowly around the room, thinly striving to search for shoes and socks, but mostly looking at the ceiling and floor.

Disgusted with their lack of enthusiasm on our vacation, I pleaded with them. "Come on, you guys! The countdown is on for Old Faithful to erupt! We're going to miss it if we don't get out there!"

Matt shot me a look that communicated *"Whatever, Mom,"* and made an unconvincing effort to pick up the pace *slightly.*

"Seriously, Matt! Claire! Let's GO! Get a move on!"

I ushered them out the door, nearly tripping over each other and our bags and backpacks and cameras. But, *ahhh.* Being at Old Faithful for that mysterious, amazing geyser eruption—something that has happened time and again through history—that was amazing to witness.

And I think my kids understood what it meant to me on that day. I think they got a glimpse of the curious student-mom—the one who looks at the world wide-eyed, heart full of wonder and awe. In that moment, they saw my enthusiasm for nature and learning.

If you asked Matt today, he'd tell you that my bent toward learning and my enthusiasm for varied experiences has led him to a greater appreciation for different cultures and people and lands. He's been more open to new experiences and realizes that they've all added color and texture to his burgeoning life. And because of my attitude toward learning, his life has been dramatically impacted.

That's how I try to approach everything. I'll rush out the door barefoot if it means I get to witness the majesty of nature. I'll lean against bookstore shelves for hours if I can find something compelling and interesting and new. I'll stay up until dawn tiptoes through the curtain of night if it means that I can spend time in solitude, watching the wonder of the midnight sky full of stars, listening for God and opening my heart to learning what that means in my life.

Learning renews me, expands my mindset, pushes back the boundaries, and demands that chalk lines be redrawn—or erased altogether.

Enthusiasm can take on many shapes and forms. It can wear many masks and even hide from you if you aren't seeking it out. But once you find it, you'll know what it is that feeds your joy and promotes enthusiasm.

For many people, it's being involved in sports or fitness. They are more enthusiastic about life after running or competing or mastering a new yoga pose.

For others, like my daughter Claire, music sets their soul soaring. Poetry communicated over guitar and piano and mandolin make the difference in their enthusiasm and joy.

Maybe for you it's baking or cooking or building with your hands. Perhaps it's planning a great party or hosting dinner in your backyard. Whatever it is, find it—and allow it to feed your joy.

Joy for life will always result in fresh enthusiasm.

And *that* is something to celebrate, no matter what the season.

17 Applause!

One Consultant Reflects on Finding Joy and Purpose with Longaberger

Longaberger is my passion.

When I heard Carol Brown utter those words, it didn't take any convincing for me to know that she was completely sincere in her admission. It's not because she's a top sponsor or a part of the $1 Million Club, or because she's a National Sales Leader or a member of the Leadership Growth Council.

It's because she has a truly inspiring sense of enthusiasm.

Carol's love for her business, for the women and men on her team, and for The Longaberger Company are as plain as the sky is blue in July. And just listening to her talk about this love—this passion of hers—spurs me on and makes me smile. Hearing Carol tell her story moves me past the office politics and legalities of business, and carries me back to the heart of Longaberger.

Fifteen years ago, Carol was working for the U.S. Post Office, delivering mail on foot. The hours spent trudging up and down country roads gave her time to think, and to contemplate her personal desires and goals. And in those days, there was much for her to think about—a lot of pondering to do.

Carol and her husband had been trying desperately to have a baby. After suffering a miscarriage and enduring the pain from such an intimate loss, she slogged through five more years of failed attempts, wondering what life would hold in store for her around the next bend.

That's when Carol began to pray for something more—something to fill the void and pour into the corners of her loneliness and disappointment. And it was within that framework of life and longing that Carol saw her first Longaberger basket. Some would say it was chance, but she knew better. Carol truly believed it was destiny.

The woman sharing her lunch table at work had two of them; and sure, they were pretty and well made from the looks of them, but Carol quickly dismissed them as unnecessary and overpriced. However, when she met yet another woman who loved Longaberger—and received an invitation to a home party—her curiosity grew. She was intrigued and had questions that prodded her insides for answers.

Soon enough, Carol was falling in love with our baskets: She adored the handcraftsmanship, the details, the way they represent a piece of American history, their beauty and quality—everything that makes them unique. *"Handmade to be handed down."* That's Longaberger. And Carol was sold.

After she began working as a Longaberger consultant, Carol found a fervor that she had never known before. She told me that she works seven days a week—*because she wants to.* She loves giving support to her new recruits and thrives on helping others become the best they can be. In fact, when I asked her what she was most grateful for in regard to her time with Longaberger, her answer was simple:

> *Sure the money is nice—I've got bills to pay! But I wouldn't even put my paycheck in the top three. What I'm most grateful for is the opportunity to be the best I can be—every day of my life, and that I can help others do the same. And I can't wait to do it!*

That kind of enthusiasm and passion cannot be learned or forced. To have a drive that fuels excitement and desire and zeal—that is inherent. That is self-motivation and enthusiasm at its best. When I have the privilege of meeting and working with people like Carol, I find my own spirits lifting—because *it's contagious!*

It reminds me of a time when Carol and I were speaking after she had completed a training. She said to me, "Tami, I got to thinking the other day, and I came up with a saying that I think really embodies what we do and why we do it."

"Oh?" I said. "I'd like to hear it!"

The words Carol spoke just seconds later spun in my ears like the compass on a time machine. "The longevity of your business," she started, "is based on the lasting relationships you build. They will help you find and meet new customers, new hostesses, or new Home Consultants—and sustain you in this business forever."

I listened, phone pressed to my ear, with silence hovering in the space between our states. I couldn't believe what she had just said—except it hadn't dawned on Carol why.

I managed to squeak out a response. "I think I've heard that before, but I can't remember where. I'll have to get back with you on that." I, of course, *did* remember where I had heard it, and from whom—but I gave way to dramatics with the knowledge that receiving a package from me would mean more to Carol than a punctuated telephone conversation.

A week or so later when the box arrived, Carol's husband Gene brought it in to her to open. Seeing the packaging on the outside, she was convinced it was Longaberger literature or the latest sales catalogs. Little did she know that waiting inside, cradled in a nest of purple tissue paper, was a simple handwritten note from me:

Great minds think alike.

—Tami

Peeling off the layers of paper from the box revealed a stone from the Dresden Homestead, bearing the imprint of one of my favorite quotes:

Your Success Will Ultimately Depend On The Relationships You Build With People.

—Dave Longaberger

Carol replayed the scene with a twinkle in her eye, beaming at the memory of something that, to me, was an ordinary gesture of kindness. But to her, *it was magic.*

Those kinds of moments are ours to create. They're opportunities to contribute to someone else's joy and gratitude, to seize situations and circumstances to create something better—to help another man or woman become a better version of themselves. It's about giving another human a piece of yourself so that your fire and spirit and devotion can raise them up. *That is a gift.* And that kind of enthusiasm is always contagious.

I am constantly on the lookout for that special sparkle—that undeniable something that sets the cheerleaders apart from the bench-sitters. What is it, exactly?

It's working hard because you want to. While accolades and prizes are meaningful, eventually they will fade and tarnish, words settling into dust. If you're really going to achieve, *you have to want it. That's* enthusiasm.

It's finding fulfillment and gratification in your days. Carol mentioned that she used to work all week just waiting for the weekend, but then by Saturday evening she'd start feeling the downward spiral of dread that Monday was quickly approaching. Now, she tells me, "Every day is a weekend doing this!" That's enthusiasm, and that truly shows that you love what you do.

It's cheering for others and sharing in their success, knowing that you'll hear the thunder of applause when it's your turn in the spotlight. Sharing in that moment and encouraging others shows that your passion for your work is genuine. Enthusiasm wants the best for everyone—and anything less is selfish ambition.

Never underestimate the power of living out your passion, shining your light, sharing your joy, and spreading enthusiasm.

If you aren't doing that now, ask yourself a few questions:

Am I truly doing something I love? If not, why? What's stopping me?

Do I believe in my company and its products or services?

How can I motivate those around me with enthusiasm? How could one small gesture be the wind in another's sails? It doesn't take much for something simple to become something profound.

Have I lost my joy along the way? When did that happen? What was I doing that crushed part of my spirit? What can I do to get it back?

Living with passion and purpose is key to loving life. Why settle for anything less than your best?

Part 5
Learning

18 Cream Pies and Ohio Buckeyes

Defying My Dad and Going to College

I can remember getting in my little 1973 green Mercury Capri and motoring the entire half-mile through the streets of Dresden to Popeye's to find my Dad. I was 17 years old, and winter was hanging on with determination, as February snow settled on the bare tree limbs and rolling hills of central Ohio. Seeing the beauty only made me more hopeful and courageous as I edited an imaginary conversation in my mind.

Easing my manual transmission into neutral, I turned the key off and forced myself from the security of the car. My boots crunched across gravel and ice until I got to the fingerprinted glass door of the restaurant. Swinging it open, I passed through, spotting my Dad immediately.

His dark, puffy eyes poured over receipts and order forms and work schedules. I studied him, noting the way his finger traced the paper in front of him. I watched his weight shift from one foot to the other, saw his brow crease as he processed what he was reading. I loved him so much. I wanted to please him. But I knew that I had to figure out how to balance two conflicting voices: stay . . . or go.

"Hi, Dad." I sucked in my breath, gathering moxie. He looked up from his work and the beginnings of a smile tugged at the corners of his mouth. "Can I talk to you, please?"

"Sure. Just a second." Passing the hostess stand, he walked to the dessert case, extracted a fresh piece of coconut cream pie, pausing only to pour steaming coffee into an ivory mug. "What's on your mind? Did you get that project done at the store I asked you about?"

"Yeah, but Dad . . . it's not about the store. I wanted to talk to you about something else."

He nodded, giving me the signal to proceed, fingers interlacing the warm cup in front of him. I fidgeted with a stray hangnail under the table and finally looked him in the face.

"Dad, I decided that I want to go to college. I've been thinking about it for a while now, and I want to study business at Ohio State in the fall."

His burly eyebrows rose predictably, and his eyes seemed to darken. I knew I was in for a most unpleasant discussion, and I realized, even then, that I was standing at a crossroads.

In some ways, perhaps most of my life had been leading up to this moment: one where I'd be forced to make a personal decision based on personal convictions, leading toward individual goals. It's not that I *wanted* to defy my father, or *wanted* to have an altercation, souring a perfectly good piece of pie. It was simply that *I wanted to follow my heart.* It was time for *my* dreams.

Fortunately for me, dreaming was encouraged in my home. Not only did I have my mother, but I also had a tough, spirited grandmother who urged me on in my pursuits. Grandma Ula Eschman grew up without the right to vote or even the right to continue working after marriage. As unthinkable as it is to us now, when Grandma and Grandpa met and fell in love at age 21, they ran away to West Virginia to get married in secret—cognizant of the fact that if others discovered their nuptials, my Grandma would no longer be permitted to teach school!

They kept their marriage quiet for two years until they finally revealed the news to the public. Talk about being courageous and following your dreams! Grandma was so committed to teaching that she would forgo a traditional wedding to save her job, provide for a budding family, and protect her dreams.

I can so clearly see looking back how fortunate I was to have had forward-thinking women in my life. There were many who would have—and *could* have—told me to just relax, settle into life next to my father, and to be thankful for that opportunity. And of course, I was! I am *entirely* grateful for my Dad; for his vision for this company, and for the legacy he left behind. But as a *woman*, I knew that I wanted and needed more than dependence on my Dad. I knew that my future required a more global, more complete skill set that would only come from absolute immersion in a diverse setting.

Unfortunately, dreams often come with a price tag—and my mother had reminded me that I would need to talk to my father about that pesky little detail. Though her love and support were boundless, her nurse's paycheck was not. So sitting down at Popeye's with my Dad meant a twofold discussion: (1) *Are you happy for me? Are you proud of me?* And (2) *Will you help me pay for this? Will you help make my dreams come true?*

A telltale nervous laughter seeped from his lips, and I could sense that we were not going to see eye to eye on the matter.

"Now Tami, *why in the world* would you want to do that? Why would you want to go to college?" He went on to inform me that "book smarts" weren't nearly as valuable as firsthand experience, and that I certainly wouldn't learn anything "practical" in college. He reminded me of all the day-to-day operations I was involved with at the Dresden IGA grocery store and highlighted the significance of my participation. Though he didn't explicitly say the words, I knew he was thinking, *"Isn't that enough for you?"*

I was crushed. I really thought my Dad would be proud of me. Instead, I found him to be disapproving and unwilling to help financially. I felt that he was judging me and critiquing my aspirations rather than sharing in my excitement. I got up and left the restaurant, pledging to Dad that I *would* find a way to pay for college. I was going to do it—with or without his help.

Thankfully, Dad eventually came around and paid the $718 per quarter for tuition. However, he also presented me with a tradeoff: I'll get out my checkbook, but you'll come to work for me for five years to pay me back.

The agreement seemed harmless enough; after all, it would be more education for me. I'd be able to learn from Dad, spend my days with him, support him as he continued to build the company, and, I hoped, strengthen our relationship.

On January 4, 1984, I reported to my first day of work—and immediately felt the slow leak of helium from my balloon of anticipation. It seemed Dad had moved my desk out into the hallway next to his office door, and I would have no space to call my own—literally or figuratively.

"I want you to sit right there for the next five years and forget everything you just learned!" he boomed.

Looking helplessly at the understated metal army workstation, I settled in, located my wilting smile—determined as ever—and did just that. I tallied and counted and analyzed amidst constant movement, workplace chatter, and phones ringing. Skirts swished past and shoes thumped by as I strove to begin a career that would validate my college degree and make my Dad proud.

After a few years, the thrill of my new job began to wane. Wanting so badly to excel and please, I said nothing for a long time. But finally, the "college repayment" had worn on me like sandpaper on maple. Offhand comments about my college experience that, to my Dad, were simply dismissive, grew increasingly bothersome. In fact, they came to feel more like an outright rebuke than playful chiding.

So the day it came up again, the dam broke. I couldn't take it anymore!

"Argh!" I yelled. Spying a basket planter out of the corner of my eye, I took aim—disregarding the fact that there was a living plant and a lot of dirt within.

"Dad, I don't want you to EVER bring up college . . . AGAIN!" And in one swift motion, I wound up and kicked that planter clear across the room! It banged with a thud into the wall, and dirt flew everywhere—scattering through the air and sending debris onto every exposed surface. I stamped out the door in a fit of anger, turning around long enough to say, "P.S.—I *QUIT!*"

And you know what? *He never mentioned it again.*

What I learned about myself during those years of "repayment" was that sometimes I needed my Dad to just be *my Dad.* I didn't want to have to "take advantage" of each moment and turn it into an object lesson. I often felt that because our time together was so limited, Dad was always trying to *teach* me something, when really, all I wanted was just *to be with him.* No lectures, no step-by-step instructions, no tutorials. Just me and Dad.

And if I had him back with me today, I'd say the same thing.

I'd tell him that I just want him. Time alone to talk. To catch up. To share in celebrations and defeats, joys and trials.

I'd ask him to sit with me over a cup of coffee and a piece of coconut cream pie . . . and just be my Dad.

19 Supporting My Kids

Why Education Is So Important to Me

As habitual travelers, I've always encouraged my kids to invite a friend along on our vacations. It proves fun for them and at the same time opens a door for me to get to know their classmates—the very people occupying and influencing their fast-changing worlds.

One of our frequent travel companions is Matt's good friend, Kurt Young; having joined us on roughly seven vacations, he is practically part of the family. In the process of getting to know Kurt, I've also had the privilege of meeting his mother, Bobbie. Over time we've developed a great friendship, and she's earned my respect for not only being a terrific mother to Kurt and his three siblings, but also for the incredible tenacity she displays in life.

Bobbie is a neonatal nurse at the OSU Medical Center where she works third shift to support her family as a single mother. Life has taught her, as it has me, that education is the key to securing meaningful work and a measure of fulfillment later in life. So I was able to laugh on the day she called me with this story—knowing that neither Kurt nor Matt would get away with such presumptuous thinking with us as their mothers—regardless of the fact that they were just seven years old at the time.

Both Bobbie and I were enduring a season of academic struggle for our boys. Perhaps it was the weather or the distraction of sports or girls; but whatever it was happened to be sinking them faster than they could kick their way to shore. Despite their youth, we were riding the boys to get their acts together—to work hard and remember that if they wanted choices in life, they'd need to study and get into college!

Yet for all of Bobbie's pleading, Kurt seemed to be unfazed by the fuss. His mother's urgency and insistence didn't compute, leaving him standing before her with eyes rolling back in his head, shoulders shrugging, dismissing her concerns.

"Kurt. You really have to start trying harder! What are you going to do if you don't get into college?!"

He stared back at her blankly, air snorting from his nose. "Don't worry, Mom! I'll just work for Matt!" he retorted in all seriousness.

Bobbie was mortified! First of all, she couldn't believe that Kurt would presume that Matt would merely waltz into a job at Longaberger, and further—that Kurt would be offered a position there on the merits of his mere identity and relationship with my son.

I still chuckle when I tell this story. It's humorous because my children have made similar comments when it comes to work and school. In exasperation they exhale loudly, complaining, "*Why do I have to hear this—again!?*"

Of course, what children don't realize is that nothing in life is certain—except change. Change is constant. Who knows what tomorrow will bring? The challenge of parenting is to prepare your kids for any number of tomorrows—any combination of great and terrible and better and worse. And doing this means starting with education.

In our house, we began discussing education early in Claire and Matt's childhood. I was an alumna and trustee at Ohio State University, so my kids were around the campus, attending games and functions from a fairly young age. For them, contemplating college was never an "if" but always a "when." I didn't approach the topic in a forceful, demanding way, by pressing my weight into debilitating thumbprints; instead, I laced conversations about their higher education with gentle expectations and matter-of-fact comments. These subtle shifts in family discussions set the precedent right away that college would be in both of their futures.

However, I also realized—and have attempted to impress upon my children—that education isn't all about "in the classroom" knowledge. I believe that raising kids is equally about being a private investigator in your own home—by observing their hobbies, promoting their strengths, and providing opportunities for growth and discovery. Doing this job well demands that good questions be asked to help them sort the grain from the chaff. It means standing beside them as they maneuver through a series of choices and decisions and come through all the stronger. It means paying attention to what makes them happy and helping them determine what they truly love—what makes their heart beat and their soul fly.

When Claire was three years old, I took her with me to the 1993 Bee. Watching the entertainment on stage, she was obviously enraptured. Twirling around in her little red dress with a red bow, she kept time with the songs and looked longingly at the entertainers. I can still see her profile in my mind as I watched the evening unfold: Locks of chestnut hair tumbling over small shoulders and onto her back, feet tapping, and tiny hands clapping. In my mind's eye, it was yesterday.

In the midst of such excitement, it didn't take long for Claire to say to me, "Mommy, I want a microphone!" So I called for a microphone, turned it off, and cut the chord at the back of the room so that she could sing her heart out—which she did, *all night long.* It was the first time I knew she wanted to perform.

In the years that followed, Claire became involved in choir and school performances, constantly seeking out opportunities to sing and to shine. It came so naturally to her, and I could see that it so obviously gave her life. She loved it and felt that she *needed it,* like a form of communication that was a direct line to her spirit. In fact, when she was 13 and we were entering that prickly domain of mother-daughter teenage sparring, I remember a time when she came to me with a song instead of a fight.

"Mom," she started, " . . . this is how I feel. This is what I want to say to you."

I leaned over the smooth kitchen countertop to insert the cassette into our nearby player. And I listened. I listened for the message that my daughter was sending me—for what she didn't know how to say with words but could express through music.

For Claire, songs are sacred; they are the poetry of the heart. And they share her heart, many times, better than spoken words.

As her best "investigator" and biggest fan, it didn't surprise me when she called home during a rough stretch of her sophomore year at OSU. She reassured me that she loved school, loved her friends and professors and everything tangible. But with such a deep connection to melody and harmony, what she missed . . . *was music.*

She told me that day how she wanted to pursue music as a career—to sing and pour her heart out on paper set alive by strings and woodwinds and voice. I told her that I would support her and do everything I could as her cheerleader, but that *she* would have to take the reins and do all the organizing and planning *herself.* If she wanted to record a CD, *she* would have to figure out how to get to Nashville. She would have to find songs to sing and rent a hotel for the week; locate a studio and band and reserve space for five days; have a photo shoot; and commit herself to working 9 AM to 11 PM in pursuit of a dream.

And I, in turn, would get out the checkbook.

I saw it as a test of sorts. I knew that if I masterminded these events, planned everything, and had a list of names at the ready, she would have nothing invested. On the other hand, if Claire was charged with the duty of locating and calling and scheduling, her fingerprints would be everywhere—and she'd be less likely to walk away. And quite honestly, I didn't think she would put forth all the effort that was required to do it.

When Claire called to tell me that all was ready and she'd be coming home to pack, I was *so* proud. She gathered her will and determination and proved to me that she had the drive to see it through; that she had the communication and interpersonal skills to get the job done. She worked the numbers, did the math, phoned her contacts, and did some networking. *Claire did it all.*

Of course, it would have been easy for me to have done it all for her. I would have simply had my assistant place a crisp itinerary inside a lovely, paisley-printed folder, passed along driving directions and a basket of cookies for the drive. That would have been simple.

But then she would have missed the lesson.

Part of education is diving into life with eyes wide open, feeling the sting of cold water, and then surfacing to revel in the glory of sun on your face. How could I have taken that from her?

I certainly have not been a perfect mom or tireless advocate for my children all of the time. But I *have* learned to be a bit more reflective about the choices I make each day, and to take the time to consider how those choices affect my kids. So if you're a parent,

I encourage you to ponder these questions while your young ones sleep peacefully.

What do I hope for the future of my children? I realize that while it is not my job to produce replicas of myself—if I want them to attend college [play an instrument, learn to cook, insert goals here], I am going to have to do something to help them arrive at the conclusion that *they* want to go to college, play an instrument, learn to cook—and so forth. How can I do so with gentleness and love?

What gifts and talents does each of my kids genuinely possess? What am I doing to nurture these gifts?

How am I encouraging their personal interests? Can I do more to help them explore possibilities?

Could I do a better job of taking a step back and letting my kids learn some life lessons without me doing everything for them—*even when it's painful and would be so much [quicker, easier, more sensible] to do them myself?*

Even if you're not a parent, I believe these questions still apply to significant people in your life. Maybe it's your partner who needs encouraging. Maybe he needs to hear that you see a spark of something special in him. Perhaps your husband has lost his job and is starting over; he needs you on the sidelines cheering! Quite possibly, yours could be the most important voice in the life of a niece, nephew, or neighbor. You can be the one who helps them dream!

Everyone needs broad horizons and the means to get to them. So help someone you love pave the way today—not by doing it *for* them, but by helping them learn to help themselves.

20 What Diversity Can Teach Us

Lessons in Tolerance

As my children can attest, one of the guiding principles I hold dear—one of the traits I strive to consistently demonstrate—is that of tolerance and acceptance of others. Something judicious deep at my core perpetually convicts me that my role in life does not include providing a rule book or even a *suggestion* book for others. I may share my thoughts and the lessons I've learned along the way—as I have in this book—but when the last sentence is written and the chapters are complete, I will walk away knowing that these are merely my experiences and thoughts. And I'll be okay if yours are different.

What I've surmised over my years on this earth is that the greater your interactions with diversity, the greater your capacity—and desire for—tolerance. Being around such a myriad of humanity—first on the oval at Ohio State University, and later during my travels—has revealed to me that we are all nomads on this journey of life. We are all seeking love and affirmation and acceptance. We strive to make meaning through faith and spirituality. We live, most of us, hoping to show kindness and find joy. Those things make us similar and give our global community common ground.

It also seems to me that tolerance and exposure are directly related: Folks who surround themselves with all walks of life tend to be a little more self-aware and softened to absolutes. Those who infrequently encounter others with different mind-sets, lifestyles, or faith practices seem to struggle a bit more with stretching their minds to accept those who don't fit neatly into a tidy, labeled box.

Part of my job as the leader of this company is to stretch people's minds. Because Longaberger's goal is to expand, I must ensure that our employees can think globally, display cultural sensitivity, and accept those walking through our doors wearing a different pair of shoes than we do. But doing so starts with small steps. And on June 6, 2008, I decided that one way to inch toward that goal was to open our doors to a group of at-risk teens from Excel Academy down the road from our corporate offices in Newark, Ohio.

Excel Academy is a not-for-profit alternative school that provides educational, mental, and behavioral support for students referred by public schools. Ninety percent of Excel's students have some form of mental health diagnosis that makes success in traditional school settings nearly impossible.

When Mrs. Abbott, one of the teachers at Excel, called our office asking if her small class of girls could come for a brief tour during an upcoming field trip, my assistant took the message and promised to set something up promptly. Knocking on my door at the Big Basket, she came in and told me of the request. She explained that this would be a group of special students from unstable homes with low socioeconomic backgrounds, and additionally, that most of them had some form of impairment.

Hearing this news made me excited! As much as the girls might benefit from seeing the wide range of opportunities available to women, *our people* would benefit from being exposed to the wide range of abilities and aspirations of our community members. It was a moment to help rearrange their boxes—make them a little less tidy and a little more messy. It was an opportunity to expand their thinking.

My assistant and I sat in my office and set about scheduling more than just the brief walk-through they requested. Our plans would take several hours and give them a real taste of Longaberger. First on the list was the boardroom: We would gather together several executives and stage a mock meeting so the girls could better understand what a business situation might look like. My assistant composed an agenda that included times for the girls to introduce themselves, hear from me, and then take the floor for questions.

Because I had recently received a touching letter from one of our consultants who was away on active duty with the military, I used our time in the boardroom to read her words of inspiration and determination to the girls. I longed to impress upon them that they could do *anything* they set their minds to. That they could be successful women running their own businesses *and* be away serving their country. That they were in the ideal position to begin to make wise choices. I was eager for them—as high schoolers with the world at their feet and options galore—to grasp hold of their personal aspirations and go after them with gusto.

With time in the boardroom quickly slipping away, we left to show the girls some key benefits to working at our corporate offices, such as free access to an on-site fitness club and the food options available at our in-house Market Basket Café.

But it was our next surprise that set the butterflies loose in my belly.

I had made arrangements for the girls and their teacher, social worker, and teacher assistant to be transported from our corporate offices to my home, Eschman Meadows, for lunch. They would be joining sales consultants from all over the country in the Garden Room. I found a stack of my Dad's books and eagerly piled them in my favorite basket. With a permanent marker at the ready, I prepared to sign each one, hoping to inspire a group of girls to dream big and believe in themselves.

Lunch provided a wonderful opportunity to get to know each of the Excel students. Stephanie Campbell, the Eschman Meadows chef at the time, came out and talked to each young woman about life as a female chef. She answered questions and took time to provide insight into her career in the kitchen. The students responded with fervor. By the end of their stay, I had discovered that their interests varied from cooking to key-chain making to dreams of having *my* job!

These were teenage girls struggling to grow up and make their own way in the world. They were battling enemies seen and unseen, fighting to escape the constraints placed on them by a diagnosis or unique family situation. They were girls who could have been my daughter, or yours; girls who could be a niece or a godchild. But instead, they're our neighbors. And they're young women who deserve a helping hand, coupled with regular doses of kindness and optimism.

For days following the "field trip," our staff members buzzed with their own thoughts and reflections. They didn't realize it at the time, but they had all learned something as they spent the day with the students of Excel. They were pulling back the curtain and peeking at the wide range of ability levels and backgrounds and family situations that make up America.

Rather than just going alone, the fact that I shared the day with my Longaberger staff meant that we now had a unifying experience in diversity. It meant that we were opening our hearts and stretching our minds to new heights and depths.

For a few brief hours that day, we forgot about the price of our shoes or the cost of our last haircut. We moved beyond petty differences and perceived ineptitudes. We overlooked the disabilities and focused on the abilities. We realized that we're all sharing the road on the same journey through life.

We're all given opportunities to show love and compassion; to demonstrate forbearance and tolerance. And to enter each day with acceptance for *all* of God's children.

How soft is your heart in this area? Are you willing to extend grace and kindness to those whose views might vary greatly from your own? Remember, tolerance doesn't necessarily mean that you *agree* with another viewpoint, or even that you have to *respect it*. However, it *does* mean that you acknowledge the freedom we all possess to make personal choices. And isn't that the great thing about our country? We are able to exercise those choices and determine our own path through this life. This journey truly is *our own*.

It's human nature to gravitate toward like-minded individuals with backgrounds that are similar to your own. However, there's something beautiful about deconstructing old walls that used to keep others out. There's greater beauty still in peeling off the outer shell of a hardened heart. What kind of condition is your heart in? Your walls?

If you are someone who needs to open up a little and invite others into your life, I urge you to do that today. I encourage you to add a little color into a world that has faded to beige. Rather than being afraid of differences, embrace them as a more accurate reflection of the kind of world in which we all live.

Embrace every stripe of our rainbow, every glinting shade on the spectrum, every human that walks before you, innately valuable, innately precious.

After all, it's not our job to judge.

It's our job to love.

21 Longaberger 101

Improve Yourself and Pass It On!

As a girl, Elizabeth McCormick was painfully shy. Her days were spent with eyes downcast, staring at dust accumulating on shoes that pinched and squeezed. Later, as a young woman, it got to the point that she wouldn't even pick up the telephone to call her hairdresser; the fear and debilitating nervousness were almost too much for her to bear. The wings of her spirit folded in on top of themselves, cloaking her in crippling timidity and suffocating introspection.

When Elizabeth joined Longaberger in 1999, she was beginning to come out of her shell but was still reserved and admits to having to push herself. I guess she figured that serving in the U.S. Army as a Black Hawk helicopter pilot would help! Elizabeth gave birth to her first child during her time *in the Army,* breastfeeding during flight school and struggling as a single parent. While she was proud to be serving our country and pursuing lofty goals, honing her technical skills and excelling as the only female in a male-dominated world left her feeling increasingly trapped on an island of isolation. She missed having girlfriends and longed for the camaraderie she knew in her hometown.

Little did she know that in the spring of 2001, a medical condition would soon send her back to the States, releasing her from active duty under a medical retirement. In Texas safely, though still healing, Elizabeth was embroiled in a bitter custody battle for her daughter.

"It was God," she told me, who protected the trajectory of her life.

Because, as we all painfully remember, that was the September that our world changed forever. After the attack on the Twin Towers that fateful autumn day, Elizabeth's old unit was deployed to Afghanistan. Had she not been sent home for her injuries, she would have lost custody of her daughter, plunging her into the depths of despair, again folding up her delicate wings.

When she had started her Longaberger business, Elizabeth told her sponsor, "Don't bother training me; I just want to have fun." She confided to me that as long as she could afford to pay for a babysitter and have fun at Longaberger parties making new friends, she was happy. She wasn't looking to begin a full-time business, choosing instead to work first a military life, then a corporate job by day, dabbling in baskets at night.

Elizabeth didn't think she needed all Longaberger had to offer—until she wore her uniform up on stage at the 2002 Bee. She had just signed two consultants to Longaberger and finally, things started to click mentally: *This business isn't about me—it's about unlocking doors for others.*

Wanting to pay it forward and help unlock doors for other women, Elizabeth continued to push herself, growing in her abilities to approach new customers with our products. She readily shared the joy and fulfillment she has found with our company and has even taught workshops multiple times at our national conventions—*opportunities she had to audition for!*

Elizabeth was struck when another consultant named Tia Wasik approached her to thank her for the difference Elizabeth's teaching had made in her life.

"Do you remember when you spoke about finding new customers at The Bee four years ago? You may not know this, but what you said really helped me; it encouraged me to get out there and get working. I thought that if you could get over your shyness and work your business so successfully, then surely I could, too. I've kept your card all these years." Reaching into her purse, Tia produced Elizabeth's Longaberger business card, edges folded and reduced to fuzz. But there it was, four years later: a testament to the power of sharing and supporting one another.

It was at that moment, Elizabeth tells me, that it all became very real to her. Her experiences in the corporate world had taught her that many people don't want to share their secrets. They hoard them, crouching to lock them in and protect them as you would a small, flickering fire from the wind. Instead, to Elizabeth's delight, she realized that Longaberger is quite the opposite.

We support. Teach. Encourage. Model. Nurture. Cheer. Train.

In short, we're a *family*.

Experiencing this love and warmth only made Elizabeth want to dive deeper into our waters. Finally, after years of struggling, she relinquished her fears, ran from the shore, and abandoned herself to the waves.

She has since been asked repeatedly to present at The Bee, most recently to share her groundbreaking progress with bridal registries, gift wrapping for customers, and filling her calendar with personal shopping appointments. She shares how she has ingeniously hired two of her best customers to help sort and distribute her product shipments, "paying" them with wonderful Longaberger baskets and pottery in return.

Guess what? They've both discovered the fun that a Longaberger career can infuse into your life, and *they've* signed up to begin their own journey with us!

In fact, the once desperately shy girl who did not have the self-confidence to make a hair appointment—the one who had just 18 team members in 2007—grew her team to *83 members* by 2009!

Against all odds, Elizabeth told me that she even shared the Longaberger experience *with her termite inspector!* He revealed to her that he's in seven to eight homes a day, and that he and his wife are looking for a way to supplement their income. Elizabeth suggested that Longaberger could be the answer they are seeking—and that if his wife ran the business, he could feel free to mention our products to all the wonderful homeowners he sees each day, avoiding a conflict of interest. (I guess there's nothing better to dull the pain of termite damage than a beautiful, new American-made basket!)

Elizabeth's transformation is a model of courage and stubborn determination. She reinvented herself to reach new heights and excel in areas she once thought lay out of reach. And we at Longaberger are *so very glad* that she kept stretching and pushing and enduring. Elizabeth models to the rest of us what it looks like to work at improving yourself . . . and then pass it on!

Ask yourself tonight—if your wings are pressed tightly to your sides and you long to use them to soar—exactly what's stopping you. Is it fear? Timidity? Worry? Something else?

Who could you invite to help you with your struggle? Who could be the cheerleader you need, applauding baby steps and celebrating each accomplishment at your side?

Are your goals and desires clearly laid out? Have you charted the path to success? Remember—*if you don't know what you want, how can you expect anyone else to help you get there?*

Don't let another day slip through your fingers. Take a deep breath, open your eyes wide to your own wonderful future, and take the first step.

You can do it!

Part 6
Family

22 Thick and Thin

Sticking Together as a Family

"Through thick or thin, you always have your family." Maybe you've heard that before. But the question is . . . do you believe it?

Stop and think about it for a moment. Let the words rest on you while you ponder what *thick* and *thin* both look like. Each of us has our own ideas, and there are certainly no right or wrong answers. Maybe a memory flashes across your mind immediately—a moment in time when your heart was broken and the comfort of your mother's hand stroking your hair was the only thing that stopped the tears coming down your cheeks.

Or perhaps your memory is filled with joy and celebration: Winning that award or being selected to represent your school or team, and wanting to pick up the phone immediately to call your husband, sister, or partner, screaming delight into the receiver.

Why is that? Where—and how—do those bonds begin?

I believe they begin at home, in the day-to-day-ness of life. I believe they begin because we're there for each other when it's happy, and also when it's not. It comes from being there when it's hard and inconvenient, when you've got a million phone calls to return and another million errands to run. Being there with nothing to say—but just *being there*.

Claire called me from college once and I realized in the midst of our conversation—even though I probably knew it long ago—that we've achieved that sort of relationship as mother and daughter. I'm sure Matt would say the same thing, but that day it occurred to me in a fresh way with Claire. Maybe it's because she's a young woman now and we can relate, in some ways, as friends. Maybe it's because I'm seeing her career begin to bloom; I'm watching her chase the dreams I first saw floating in her eyes years ago.

Claire was telling me about how she had just set up her MySpace music page—and she was positively effervescent. Listening to her chatter on, I felt the exhilaration creep over the line, and was overcome with pride. My little girl, all grown up . . . and a *singer!*

Being there for her in the good times is the reward for going through the bad times together, as well. Because I'm sure you'd all agree: If someone doesn't stick with you through the muck and mire, they sure won't be on your short list when it's time to celebrate.

In the summer of 2007, Claire was thrilled to be voted senior captain of her high school soccer team. Overjoyed with the title, she vowed to work even harder than usual, serving as a leader and a key player for the team. With wind in her sails and sun on her shoulders, she viewed her final year as a great uncharted course stretching out in front of her, ready for exploration, and filled with the kind of dreams that make high school magical.

The morning of August 17 began just like any other. We pulled our chairs up to the round wooden breakfast table in the kitchen, spooning cereal into hungry mouths and commenting on Al Roker's weather forecast. The cat threaded itself over feet and between legs, craving our attention and our caress. Soon enough the discussion shifted to the events of the day, and Claire reminded me of her soccer scrimmage later that afternoon.

"Don't forget, Mom—it's our *last* scrimmage before the regular season starts! You'll be there, right?"

"Of course I'll be there! *Don't worry.*"

She gulped down the last of her milk, wiped her mouth with the edge of her napkin, and bent over, kissing my cheek and giving me a quick squeeze. "Love you, Mom."

"I love you, too, honey." She walked across the kitchen and disappeared through the doorway, shoes padding down the hall until a door shut behind her, drowning out all sounds of Claire.

Claire had played soccer practically since she started losing teeth; her love for and devotion to the game course through her blood as though part of her very anatomy. As with Matt's love for golf or mine for the outdoors, her sacred bond with soccer was central to her identity and personal energy. So the prospect of being a team captain—*during her senior year*—was not only a special honor; it was potentially the single most memorable sporting experience of her high school career.

I arrived at her scrimmage that afternoon in time to find a seat on the bleachers and observe the pregame warm-ups. Claire dribbled the ball with speed and grace. I could see how excited she was to play in the scrimmage, ushering in a season of new potential and, we hoped, victory!

But midway through the first half, though everything had been glittering and full of promise, ominous clouds marched across our blue skies, beckoning tidal waves to crash in their stead. With my smile washing quickly away, I watched in horror as

Claire went down, screaming in agony with her knee splayed out sideways on the freshly mowed field below.

I felt myself battle against seat-riveting fear and the powerful urge to run to my daughter as she lie on her back staring at the sky, hands desperately clutching clumps of grass, fighting back pain and overwhelming fear of what was happening to her.

Deciding to let the trainers move in to swiftly assess the situation, I watched from the sidelines, terrified and experiencing the kind of heartbreak that only a mother can know: Something was really wrong. She was *really* hurt. Little did I know that this event would affect far more than soccer that year: Claire would lose her entire senior year of soccer *and* forfeit her final basketball season as well.

She had completely destroyed her ACL and severely torn her MCL in her left knee.

She was, as one can imagine, *completely* devastated. Her world grew flat and colorless. So many dreams would be left on the shelf, open to the dangerous "what-if's" and "maybe's." It was one situation I couldn't fix for her. I couldn't call up a friend or ask a favor. I couldn't restart the day, demanding the sun retrace its fiery steps, giving us another chance at glory instead of defeat. But what I could do was be there for Claire. I could make sure she knew that—as far as I was concerned—the world stopped in that moment.

Not long after the injury, Claire and I went to a specialist in Columbus who recommended a couple weeks of rehab prior to surgery so that her knee would be strengthened and as healthy as possible before correction.

And this is where the "thick and thin" part comes in: To adhere to the rigorous rehab prescription, Claire and I had to drive to Columbus three times a week . . . for *six months.*

Of course, as a mother, I was so happy to be with her. I put life on hold to drive her the hour and 15 minutes from Dresden to Columbus—to talk with her about teachers and homework and boys, to discuss college and dream about her future at OSU. And to enjoy the hour-and-fifteen-minute drive from Columbus back home to Dresden.

As a businesswoman, and company leader, however, spending this time with Claire was a little more of a sticky situation. Leaving the office multiple times a week at 2:30 or 3 o'clock meant walking out on loose ends, closing my computer, manipulating travel times, and exiting meetings early. It meant tossing a flurry of papers into a basket, grabbing my phone and planner, and sitting in the car, working behind the steering wheel while Claire worked behind weights and treadmills inside. It meant sacrificing.

But sacrifice comes with the territory when we're talking about "thick and thin."

Claire did recover. Although she missed both sports seasons and had to revamp her senior-year ideals, we were grateful for a successful outcome that has enabled her to play both casual sports with friends and intramurals at Ohio State.

Emotionally, there was never a choice to be made in regard to Claire's rehab. I wouldn't have imagined missing it—the thought never would have even entered my mind! I'm proud to have walked through those dark, churning waters with my daughter; to have been the face she saw between drops of sweat and tears. I'm proud to have *been there*.

Yet intellectually, the choice demanded some thought. Working in a car in between long drives isn't terribly conducive to making difficult decisions and keeping the framework of scope and sequence clear. It isn't all that convenient to balance a notepad over your car horn. *But* when we're talking thick and thin, *you do it anyway.*

Think back on your life for a moment. Maybe your story is filled with *Leave It to Beaver*–like episodes of support and nurturing. Maybe your mother sashayed into the living room with cookies every day after school. Maybe your father was there with a firm but loving hand, guiding you to adulthood with faith in your safe arrival.

However, it's more likely that your story had a few Eddie Haskell moments that left you awash in dilemmas and uncertainty. We've all been there—left to pick up the pieces of something that wasn't supposed to end the way it did. And then what?

Was anyone there with you, reaching for a broom and dustpan? Was there another hand in yours, another voice to counsel you?

The great thing about life is that—despite setbacks and disappointments—we are always given a new day. And while our childhoods shape us all profoundly—even in ways we don't always recognize or want to acknowledge—*you can choose to leave it behind you and start over.* Whether you had Beaver's picket fences or Eddie's rotten luck, each day is a fresh start. We are offered the unbelievable opportunity to make of it what we wish. That alone is reason for celebrating!

If you are spending today lamenting yesterday—or last year— I encourage you to turn the lens away from *them* and *their choices* and how *they wronged you,* and turn it to yourself. Give the power of joy and choices and happy tomorrows back to *yourself.*

Take the first step by answering a few questions:

How can I show the loved ones in my life today that I will always be there for them?

What would it look like for me to truly sacrifice for another? Am I willing to do that?

What message would it send [*insert name*] to see me drop everything for him or her?

Do I believe in thick in thin? Or have I been quick to run the other way? Why?

How could my choices restore health to a hurting relationship?

Lastly, if you've been impacted by someone taking the backseat for you and you've never expressed your appreciation, sit down right now with your favorite ink pen and some pretty paper and make your thoughts tangible. Thank them for staying near when others felt far off. Thank them for the gift of *presence*. Thank them for crying with you and holding you tight; for demonstrating their love *with action*.

Thank them for thick and thin.

23 Memory Making

How Family Traditions Became Our Glue

For some families, it's riding bikes to the ice cream shop every Tuesday evening in summer, passing the same landmarks and street signs, pondering the flavor they'll order and whether they want rainbow or chocolate sprinkles. For others, it's reading books after dark while piled in cozy PJs on the sofa, rain smearing the vista through foggy windowpanes. For still others, it's the annual tradition of picking a bouquet of flowers for the birthday girl, helping her celebrate another year reigning as family princess.

Whatever the traditions are in your home, I'm guessing you'll agree with me when I say that I believe family traditions are the glue that holds us all together. When life spins away from us and just sitting down for dinner becomes an Olympic undertaking, it's comforting to know that we have the backdrop of traditions binding us together.

In our family, the glue we grab for most often consists of backpacks and lakes and hiking. Travel was, and continues to be, central to our understanding of each other and our appreciation for the world around us. It has always unlocked my heart in mysterious ways, helping me to fall deeper into myself. Travel helps me remember who I am and what I believe; it allows me to connect with my spirit and with my children.

In addition to strengthening these bonds, the luxury I've been afforded to travel the country and world has helped me to better express my love for nature and all its intricacies: birds and trees, fields and forests. It opens the door to teachable moments with my children where I can point out the exquisite nuances of different cultures—reminding them that none is better, none is worse; rather, all are beautiful in their uniqueness.

On each trip, we get the chance to meet a myriad of people with varied lifestyles and socioeconomic backgrounds. These encounters exhibit a wide spectrum of privilege, poverty, different foods, ways of life, beliefs and understandings of the world. Travel provides families with a global classroom—and *that* is priceless.

Some of our favorite trips have been to the U.S. national parks. We treasure the rustic, untethered beauty that has been preserved for all to enjoy. And while it may sound cliché to admit, my kids and I all agree: After at least three visits, Yellowstone is still our favorite. Claire recalls leaving the park and traveling through Big Sky, Montana, filled with the kind of awe that comes from experiencing something so huge and wonderful—something beyond words or snapshots. It inspired Matthew to want to visit all of our national parks in his lifetime, a goal which he's well on his way to reaching!

Even when we're not traveling, we still do our best to intentionally spend time together. I often plod over the back hill of our home to scout mushrooms with Claire, or spend the afternoon with both kids bundled up at OSU football games. We look forward to those times because we truly enjoy *being together* without any other distractions. I worked hard in my children's formative years to make our time as a family *fun*—to make our outings something they'd look forward to, even if they weren't extravagant or showy.

Growing up with my own mother taught me valuable lessons about enjoying life without frills. Instead, we added our own every Christmas by decorating homemade gingerbread houses. This tradition continues to this day in my own home, thanks to my mother Laura's tireless work. She mixes up the batter, rolls out large sheets of gingerbread [no graham cracker houses for us!], sequesters them in the oven, and then puts the houses together for us with homemade icing. We can barely concentrate on the decorating with so many forms of deliciousness overtaking our kitchen!

When Mom finishes the houses, we all get to work adding frosting, sprinkles, candy, licorice laces, marshmallows—anything we can find that will pass for "decoration." Claire still scolds me for my efforts a few years ago to make a "healthy" gingerbread house. Apparently, she decided that organic ingredients were not part of this tradition, and almonds would no longer be considered appropriate for home detailing. *(Who knew?)* It's possible she just made up these particular rules to squash my creativity, since I have a hidden talent for shaping ridiculously creative gingerbread houses. That's okay; I'll stick to baskets and save the almonds for my afternoon snack if it means sharing a fun afternoon with my family!

The fun part about gingerbread houses for me nowadays is that my kids invite their friends to come over and be part of our family for the day. We line up a virtual neighborhood on the kitchen counter—a subdivision in the making—and quickly impose our construction and design ideas. We laugh and listen to Christmas music with lights twinkling around us and the warmth of the oven setting our hearts aglow. It's probably the closest I've ever come to Norman Rockwell in my life, and I love it. Not because it's Norman Rockwell, but because it's *us*. It's our family—imperfect and messy, but full of love and joy, bound by a decades-old tradition that continues to glue us together with sweetness and dreamy wonder.

What are you doing today with your loved ones to add some glue to your relationship? While holidays are certainly a good place to start, don't let the calendar dictate when you get together! With a little effort, you can form traditions with your family that will make the entire year special.

Maybe a "date night" with your son or daughter during which they reveal their report card would be an easy first step in establishing meaningful traditions. Planting a tree each fall with your spouse or partner might be a special reminder of another year together; those seedlings will eventually grow deep roots and become a beautiful symbol of your love and commitment.

Whatever you decide to do, resolve to make the effort. Resolve to be proactive. Find a way to celebrate days that seem ordinary— and together, make them *extraordinary*.

24 The Best Medicine

Laughter Is Critical for Any Family

Out my kitchen windows, I could see the sun slide lazily down the evening sky like a pad of butter across a hot griddle, coming to rest behind the trees near my home. I love those quiet moments of beauty and predictability; in some ways it's comforting to know that I can depend on the coming and going of daylight and dusk and the turning of seasons.

Muffled chatter floated in from voices in the other room. I poured a glass of wine and took the bottle to share with my friends, heading into the living room and settling into a cozy circle of leather chairs. The conversation began with regular pleasantries, football picks for the fall, college recruiting practices, jokes, and easy banter. Soon enough, my son Matt joined us, looking all handsome and grown up, and it brought me back to his childhood and all the many fun and spontaneous things we used to do.

"Matt," I asked. "What do you remember about growing up? What's one of your favorite memories?"

Without a second's hesitation he looked up and declared, "Food fights with Grandpa."

"What?" our visitor chuckled. "Tell me about those food fights!"

"Well, we would go over to Grandpa's house for lunch on Sundays and have Kentucky Fried Chicken," he began. "And usually by the end of the meal, he'd be flinging drumsticks and dinner rolls at one of us. Either that or he'd load up his spoon with mashed potatoes, pull it back, and launch it right in someone's face. That was Grandpa."

We were all rolling at the thought of the mess! I remember times, if I wasn't careful, that I'd get pelted in the side of the head with something and have to scramble to retaliate. Let me tell you—when my Dad wound up and threw a biscuit, he threw *hard!* We would have corn, cole slaw, drumsticks, and dressing smeared all over the dining room floor. The table would be covered in food—and we'd be clutching our bellies, rolling with laughter, and pointing at the poor soul who ended up with ears covered in slop.

My father always was a prankster. He always loved finding an excuse to embarrass Rachel or me, or get our kids dirty. Both Matt and Claire remember their birthdays well: Blowing out the candles and promptly feeling Grandpa's hand on the back of their heads, smashing their faces into a pile of frosted confection. Little Matt was only five years old when Dad died, but Dad made such an impression on him that to this day, at 18, he'll recount the cake and KFC incidents with a smile spread wide on his face.

This kind of environment taught me that laughter can lighten anyone's load—except, perhaps, Rachel's and mine when *we* got stuck cleaning up the mess! Dad relied on silliness and whimsy to remind us all not to take life too seriously. Too much work might be okay; but work without laughter could kill anybody. At Longaberger, we still say, "Around here, a sense of humor is mandatory." Dad's perspective on laughter, practical jokes, and humor in general left a powerful impression on me. It's impacted my approach to work, friendship, and as a mother parenting my own kids.

Claire and I have a fun ritual every time we hear that great Motown classic, "Ain't No Mountain High Enough," by Marvin Gaye and Tammi Terrell. It's hard to remember how our little dance even got started, but it's a special connection that we share even now that's she's away at college. If I hear the song on the radio, I'll call her or send a text message letting her know that I'm thinking of her, wishing she were in the car with me to stick her hands out the sunroof and shake her arms together with mine. If she hears the song, she'll call me to say she's waving her hands down on the floor and wishing I could be next to her doing the same thing.

If you were to drive past us on some Ohio road and saw Claire and me waving and wiggling and laughing, I'm sure you'd think we were nuts! But I think that laughter is a great way of gaining perspective and bonding with your kids. We toss our heads back and enjoy the feeling of memories in the making. We bask in the moments that are unplanned, serendipitous events of the heart.

I may not be a jokester in the same way my father was, but I purposefully surround myself with people who make me laugh and have a positive energy. Whether laughter comes by not taking yourself too seriously or by making faces collide with birthday cake—it can help to relieve stress and regain an even keel.

Could it be that you're reading this and you don't *remember* the last time you had a good laugh? I mean a *really* good laugh— the kind that leaves your stomach hurting and you gasping for air. What can you do to relax a little and enjoy the silly moments that come your way?

One thing that I've had to stop and take inventory of are the people who fill my life. While I'm certainly not suggesting that you forsake your friends, you have to ask yourself: Are you spending too much time with those who drag down your spirits? Are you allowing them to sap your energy and your steal your joy? Perhaps it's time to be more intentional about spending time with those who fill you, feed your energy, and lighten your load.

After all, life's too short to stay buttoned up and grim-faced all the time. Sometimes the best response might just be to throw a biscuit or two. And *laugh* about it.

25 Expanding My Family

Opening Doors for Longaberger Consultants

My Dad was a master at opening doors and welcoming others. He had a way about him, a witty gleam that drew people in and made them want to work hard, please him, and become a part of his family. What they didn't know was that he considered them family the moment they first walked through the door of the Longaberger Company.

My father and I always believed that relationships are at the heart of any business. We work tirelessly to maintain those we've already established, while discovering and nurturing new ones along the way. In the mid-1990s, when we were building baskets faster than we ever imagined, we invested in our employee relationships tangibly by throwing elaborate company picnics that would make even Elvis burn with jealousy.

These "Family Days," as Dad called them, were filled with carnival rides and cotton candy, hamburgers and hot dogs, stuffed animals and sugary treats galore. Longaberger employees arrived, hand-in-hand with their families, and ate and played all day long. I have so many wonderful memories of bringing my own children to those events when they were small; memories of twirling on rides under puffy clouds with Dad nearby, or watching Claire and

Matt toss rings in hopes of winning another prize. Dad filled up on joy by watching others laugh and enjoy his generosity. It was one of his favorite parts of our business year.

Soon enough, however, with the business growing and our numbers of employees exploding, Dad decided that we would need more space—something a little *bigger*. Working in secret, he stayed late for countless nights while planning his most memorable Family Day ever. Then, in early spring on the day before local amusement park Cedar Point officially opened—flinging wide its entrances to thrill seekers everywhere—the Longaberger caravan descended on it like a battalion of picnic ants ready to devour crumbs. Dad had rented out the *entire* park!

Kids lit out in all directions, shoes ready to spontaneously combust from friction, speed, and sheer will to be the first on the Demon Drop. They raced between a maze of metal bars meant to organize hundreds of impatient riders, and climbed stairs leading up to the embarking zone. With clammy hands and pounding hearts, Longaberger children strapped in and screamed their way to a smiling, happy end.

Then they got off and did it again. *And they never waited in line.*

Even after Dad passed away in 1999, our company rocketed like a shooting star. We grew 25 percent each year and hurdled closer to our $1 billion year of 2001. We could afford to not only *provide* our employees with a company picnic; we could *lavish* them with a Disney-like getaway full of surprises and fun.

I still think of those sweet, carefree Family Days and wish that our budget allowed for them to continue. Making the decision to cut back on things like Cedar Point and free stuffed animals was excruciating for me, because I knew all too well how much those gestures meant to our employees and their families. But I also knew that maintaining the longevity of our company—and thus keeping the jobs of literally *thousands* of people—was more important than Ferris wheels, cotton candy, and hamburgers.

Changes bring growing pains, and this change was indeed painful. Both the economic downturn that started affecting us after 2002 and the cuts that followed—picnics and all—stung and burned, leaving scars that continue to heal to this day.

However, as we've changed, we've been able to get more creative and resourceful, slowly reinstating some of those social activities. In recent years, we've had movie nights at corporate headquarters and sponsored huge annual fishing tournaments attended by over 500 people. And each year at Christmas, our employees have the opportunity to receive a special basket designed and produced just for them.

I relish the opportunity to give back to our employees by providing free fitness centers and health-related classes that help with issues like diabetes, substance abuse, elder care, anger management, and others. We strive to remind members of the Longaberger family that our company is built on people and the relationships we have with each other.

Another exciting opportunity that I love to promote among our sales team and customers are our Eschman Meadows Midday Gatherings. As a special outing created for our salespeople only, I open up my home for guests to come and enjoy lunch in my Garden Room. If I happen to be home during these gatherings, it's a pleasure for me to pop in, sign baskets, and get to know more of our extended family.

What I find on those days as I talk more and more with our sales consultants—especially the young women—is just how *grateful* they are for the opportunity to work the hours that best accommodate their families, to be in charge of their own paycheck, and—for many of them—to have the *option* to stay home with small children. It's deeply gratifying for to me to hear that they feel as blessed by Longaberger as I do. Sure, our daily lives may be different on paper or in pictures, but when you get down to matters of the heart, we really *aren't* that different.

I should note that when I talk about "opening doors" for Longaberger family members, I'm not speaking only in a literal sense. The longer I've been living in this world, the more important it's become for me to figuratively open doors for others, and to "expand my family" beyond those one might expect to find at a suburban-neighborhood Longaberger party. For that reason, it's been exciting for me to welcome a growing number of men into our family as new consultants.

Some of them have been around for quite a while; and one in particular has become a dear friend to me. After joining Longaberger as a Home Consultant, Benno Landfair has gone on to really grow his personal business, now as a Branch Leader. With the help of his partner, David Petersen—who is also a Branch Leader, and helps Benno oversee their home office—Benno has built a successful company that he cherishes. He recently shared with me that he is motivated by the rewards that Longaberger offers, and even more so, because of the friendships he and David have made over the years.

Quite some time ago I was in Kansas City meeting with a group of consultants when Benno revealed to me his affection for Ohio State football. Of course, I was immediately charmed by this admission. I listened attentively as he went on to explain that he was originally from Columbus, and that David is an OSU alumni. So that fall I invited them both to join me at a Buckeye football game—and we had a ball!

Knowing how much Benno had enjoyed the day at the "Horseshoe" and our time together, I called him up a few months later and asked if he'd like to go to another game with me. I could hear him pause on the other end of the line, hesitating for some reason.

"Tami, I would love to go," he replied—but then explained, "but you just took me last year, and I think if I go again you should make me work for it."

I'll admit that I was more than a little surprised. "Okay," I said. Stopping to think for a moment, I continued with the charge. "You sell $300,000 this year, and we'll go to another football game. Who do you want to see them play?"

"USC."

"Done. You sell $300,000, and we'll go see Ohio State play USC."

So for the next several months leading up to The Bee, I watched Benno's numbers. Not daily, or even weekly, but I checked in with him and tried to keep a pulse on how he was coming. And do you know what? He not only sold $300,000—but he did it *with a month to spare.*

I was so excited for him that I picked up the phone to congratulate him as soon as I heard the news. When Benno tells the story of his accomplishment, he shares not just what it meant for me to call him—but how gratifying it was for him to have tens of other consultants and Branch Leaders reach out to him and share in his joy and accomplishment.

Benno is Longaberger's first male to become the number-one sales leader in the history of our company. He's setting the stage, we hope, for many more men to feel inspired and motivated to do the same. Knowing how extraordinarily hard he had worked to get to that place—and in recognition of this groundbreaking feat—I decided to do something special for him. I had one of our weavers construct a one-of-a-kind basket for him: A small, round, black-and-white bowl to match his living room at home. I signed the bottom, "Benno—Dreams do come true. –Tami"

And Benno is living proof of that assertion. He is proof that hard work and determination will take you straight to the top. He is proof that you *can* reach your goals. And he is proof that at Longaberger, we strive to treat everyone like they're part of our family.

Last year, Benno earned a spot on our company cruise, an incentive program toward which our sales force works—both in sales numbers and sponsored recruits. However, one of our rules is that if a Longaberger consultant wants to take a guest, it must be his or her spouse.

While the rule may be well intentioned (to prevent one consultant from taking another, versus each one *earning* a spot), we ran into a snag with Benno. First, despite the fact that he is in a long-term, loving, committed relationship, since his relationship is not "legally recognized," our written rules seemed to exclude his partner from the cruise. Secondly, David is *also a consultant.* Benno sat with the presumption that with two strikes against him, he would be traveling alone.

However, I didn't feel that Benno's accomplishments should have been celebrated alone, without his partner of so many years to join him in the spotlight. And while there are people who will differ with me on this point, I don't believe that it's my job to referee the lifestyle of another human, much less someone who had done so much for the company. How could I deny Benno his best friend and partner? How could I set him afloat in the Caribbean with David at home alone?

So we made it a non-issue. David was able to go because we *chose* to value our sales family over a published rule that would only serve to discriminate in his situation. When we were on the boat and our consultants received an invitation, I made certain that David's name was mentioned so he would not be left out or overlooked. As we planned dinner or considered table arrangements, those considerations always included both Benno *and* David. And to this day, when I send a written note or put a letter in the box for Benno, the name of his partner is written right next to his own.

At Longaberger we believe that you are valuable because *you're you.*

That's what you do for family. That's how you open doors. That's how you rise above and *accept your family for who they are:* Ever-changing, ever-expanding, *but always your family.*

Part 7
Courage

26 Learning to Pull Myself Up

Finding Courage Within

I was 12 years old when my parents separated, and 17 when they eventually divorced. Whether the strain in their relationship stemmed from too many days spent traveling in opposite directions or too many nights existing in silent isolation, I'll never know. And to be honest, it doesn't matter to me anymore.

While divorce is never easy or desirable, there are times, I suppose, when it seems preferable to yelling and fighting and general ugliness. Luckily for my sister Rachel and me, our home was quiet and respectful, with none of the aforementioned noisy pain. Yet there was a certain deadness—a nondescript lack of love that produces raw uneasiness. An unsettling tension in the air that, while not loud or injurious, was unhealthy nonetheless.

And that's what our home was like during the years leading up to my parents' separation. I could sense that things were somehow "off." I could see it in my mother's eyes and could feel it when my hands touched the couch, warm and rumpled in the morning. And I understood that I was to step carefully, avoiding land mines and eggshells constantly. It was a tiring time that, to be completely honest, I was *glad* to see come to an end.

But having Dad out of the house meant new struggles for me; new longings for the little girl who only wanted her father's unconditional love, attention, *and time*. I was so desperate to please him, to have my victories lock his eyes and grab his chin, forcing him to look. *To look at me and notice me.* While this would come later, it was a deep need at that time—biting at my heels like an unrelenting hound. I would spend years furiously trying to shake it.

While I was busy running from imaginary hounds, my Dad was busy running three successful businesses: his restaurant, Popeye's; the Dresden IGA grocery store; and a drugstore. These establishments became the heart of our town and allowed my Dad to make a living. I was older then, and grateful for Dad's provision, but as with everything in life, it came with a cost. He was so preoccupied, living and working beyond the reach of my teenage fingers.

In the mid-1970s, Dad asked my grandfather to make a sampling of baskets to sell at the Dresden IGA on a small display area at the end of one of the aisles. Orders came pouring in and I saw that familiar but unwelcome sparkle in his eyes: He wanted more. My head was spinning and my heart pounded for a piece of him. How could he possibly keep up with yet *another* business? I knew the answer and what it would mean for Rachel and me. And I felt the splintering again.

Finding the capital for a *fourth* venture meant that something had to go. Dad had already mortgaged the house that my mother, Rachel, and I lived in *three times* to pay for his business gambles, so he knew that another mortgage was out of the question. He paced the floor, massaging his forehead with one hand while the other pressed into his waist.

With the rest of life blending beige into the background, baskets became the makings of my father's wishes and dreams. He saw the adoration of customers when they picked up his family's craft, and heard praise fall down like rain on his head. Yet despite the many baskets made and sold, his fledgling business just couldn't seem to stay above water. He couldn't locate quite the right fit or function. And instead of being buoyed by hope, it was drowning in uncertainty and lack of direction.

And so, Dad took a step back and examined the pawns on his chessboard. Popeye's. The drugstore. The grocery store. A potential basket company?

I knew that Dad believed in his baskets and in the talent of the craftsmen and women helping him make them. I also knew he wanted to produce quality, American-made crafts that could stand the test of time and put Ohio to work.

Rather than selling the drugstore and absorbing the profit to help the baskets—or reduce basket offerings at Popeye's to increase financial gain—my father did something most people would not have the guts to do: He sold all three *profitable businesses* and poured every red cent into the drowning basket company that he *hoped* could survive. He sacrificed it all for Longaberger: Proven avenues of income, proven successes—gone overnight, to fund one man's dreams.

In hindsight, of course, I can admire and applaud this decision. After all, nothing great comes without risk. But let's be honest. It *was* a somewhat financially irresponsible move to make, considering he had two daughters to help support and three mortgages to pay off. In fact, it was *very risky!* Yet at the same time, it was an incredibly courageous display of steadfast devotion to his dreams and fidelity to the inner compass telling him to *"go for it."*

I don't know if I would've made that choice were I in his shoes; it's hard to say. But I am forever grateful for the chance to have witnessed my Dad paving the way to his own American Dream. I saw him pull himself up by his bootstraps and *make the dream happen*. He didn't sit around and wait for something magical to float in through the window; he *made it happen* at considerable potential risk to himself and his family.

By the time I had to harness my own piece of courage, I was old enough to realize that my sacrifices and difficulties were quite different from those my Dad encountered. It's true that I wasn't handed anything; my Dad made sure I earned everything that entered my world. At the same time, working for Dad and gaining an understanding of the business was different from remortgaging one's home or selling three successful businesses. So although I saw these traits in my father at a young age, I didn't realize then that making the choice to pull myself up—to locate my own courage—would look so different and still be so hard.

I remember one particularly poignant evening while I was a student at Ohio State. For all my studying and earnest effort, seeing red ink on my test added to an already-bad day and delivered a clear message: I had not performed to the level I had come to expect from myself. I had let myself down and soon felt the clouds of frustration and self-pity looming.

Returning to my dorm room, I tossed my keys, jacket, and book bag on my bed, allowing them to drop with the kind of weight that occupied my stomach. The heaviness of disappointment hung over me like a thick woolen canopy, and I realized that I didn't want to be alone. I wanted my Dad. I wanted the kind of comfort that comes from home, from familiarity, from someone who loved me no matter how badly I had messed up, from strong arms wrapped around me.

So I called him. "Dad. I've had such a rotten day. Will you come over and just sit with me? Have dinner with me?"

His response, though gentle, was a rebuke for which I was not at all prepared. Looking back, I suspect he must have had a bad day himself. "You want me to do what?"

I hesitated, shoulders sagging, knowing how busy he was, trying to grow this company and fend off a myriad of other demands.

"I want you to come over. I need to see you tonight."

"Tami, I'm not coming over tonight." He sighed, exhaling loudly into the phone. "You're going to have to learn how to pick your own self up. Because there's going to be a time that I'm not going to be there, and that's when you're going to need me the most. And you need to learn how to reach behind and lift yourself up."

"Okay, Dad." I cradled the phone, lingering over it with eyes swimming. Placing my hand on the wall, I let my head drop, tears sliding down my cheek. I was so disappointed with his response. He let me down again—right when I *really* needed him.

I wanted to sit on the bench and take myself out of the game. Let someone else stretch their muscles and endure the tiring workout; let someone else do the hard work.

But in spite of my despair at the time, I realize now that my Dad taught me a valuable lesson that night. He knew that if I always depended on someone else to prop me up, to help me "fix" a bad day, that I'd never be the strong woman I am today—that I'd never be able to lead a company or handle the brunt of impossible corporate decisions.

Now mind you—my father was not preaching that every man or woman is an island, nor was he insinuating that we should eschew the support that comes from family and loved ones. But in that moment, he had the wisdom to see that I needed to pull myself up, to straighten my spine and breathe deeply. Sure, college can be tough and the days grow long; but I was not in crisis. I was not truly suffering or dealing with tragedy or emergency.

What felt urgent to me was really an opportunity for me to be develop a sense of personal courage. And although I didn't realize it until many years later, that night was a watershed moment: Just as there is room for vulnerability and intimacy in life, there are times for strength and independence as well. It takes courage to exhibit these qualities; and even though it's hard sometimes to get off the bench and get into the game, *no one ever wins by sitting on the bench.*

Perhaps you feel right now as though you're sitting on the bench, watching life pass you by. What small changes could you make today that would fuel bigger changes down the road? Maybe you have to start with the commitment to take better care of yourself. To get out and take a walk, enjoy the beauty of nature, and treat your body with an added measure of kindness.

Maybe you have to find the courage to trust yourself a little more; to listen to your gut when it urges you to leave your abusive relationship, or trust your heart when it tells you that you deserve better. Perhaps you need to believe your friends when they tell you that they'll be there for you, loving you, helping you find those bootstraps again.

Or maybe you have to give some honest thought to your job and career path. Are you really happy? If I produced a crystal ball and told you that you'd be sitting in the same cubicle, talking to the same people in 15 years, would you be energized . . . or depressed? What can you do about that?

What hurdles lie in your path in the way of finding your courage? What steps would you have to take to remove those hurdles; or if they can't be removed, to learn to jump them?

One of the hurdles I needed to overcome in finding my own courage and realizing that although my father loved me, I couldn't depend on him to always be there for me—to be *present* during times that felt hopeless. Sure, I could pick up the phone anytime to talk to him, but we all know that sometimes hearing a voice is just not enough. Sometimes you need arms and hands and a body.

Never did I feel this so palpably than in the weeks and months after Dad died, because then, of course, I could not call him. I could not meet him for dinner. I could not look forward to his reassurance at work and his listening ear during my struggles. I could only sit quietly with my memories of those times. And *that*, at times, felt nearly unbearable.

Whether it was the divorce or the businesses or his drive to dream and create, my Dad was a busy man. Getting over my need for his validation and recognition was a major feat for me. And it took a lot of courage to be my own person; to love Dad and to value our relationship, but to *pick my own self up*.

He showed me how to do it when he sold everything, and I saw that. He showed me what it looked like to be a courageous dreamer, and I understood that. He taught me how to find that unwilling part of your hands that does the picking up, and he showed me how to put that part to work.

After all these years of watching and seeing and understanding, I am proud to say that today, I am a witness to his courage . . . and to mine.

27 Empty Shoes at The Bee

Finding Courage in Loss

It's funny how even the best-laid plans, the most articulate set of directions, can still leave you scrounging in the dust for a map. The mind is a funny thing that way; it tricks you into comfort and steadiness, into feeling prepared and ready and standing on solid ground.

But sometimes there's no map to follow. Sometimes there aren't even roads built yet for where life wants to take you. That's what I discovered when my Dad was diagnosed with cancer in June 1997.

Aside from the emotional implications of such news, this kind of impending loss threw a myriad of questions into the air about the future of Longaberger. Like feathers escaping a down pillow, questions were ubiquitous that summer, floating around us and settling gently on our shoulders. We didn't yet feel their heaviness, but we felt the weight of their reality, and that was enough.

As summer's vibrant greenery drained into the flaming colors of fall, Dad and I began to connect more every day. We talked for hours about everything, leaving no stone unturned as we moved through life and legal and accounting issues. We had candid conversations about the business and about what it would look like going forward. We began working on planning his estate. And perhaps most importantly to me, we became closer than we ever had before, finding common ground, love, and forgiveness. It was a rich time of sharing I will cherish forever. Those 18 months of slowing down and coming together gave us a chance to renew a relationship that had once been hurried and neglected—and for that I am grateful.

In August 1998, I was 37 years old and serving as the president of Longaberger. It was then, after having worked in the business for 16 years, that Dad added "CEO" to my job description. I suppose in some ways it was an expected move—a passing of the torch. I had been at Dad's side through all kinds of ups and downs in the company, piping up with opinions and numbers and advice. So I certainly felt ready to *manage*.

But what I didn't know then is that *leading* is an entirely different thing.

It would take five years after Dad's passing before I could fully wrap my mind around the transition I was undergoing. Before he was gone and our plans existed only on paper, everything seemed sensible. Pragmatic. Seamless. Moving through life would be neatly wrapped up, thanks to the hard work we had put in during the year and a half leading to his untimely death. But how could I have known how it would feel to sit behind his desk and drive this ship without him? Would I be able to move forward without him to guide me?

By the time I went to the Longaberger National Convention (called "The Bee") in July 1999, Dad had been gone for five months. I had never attended a Bee without him—and I had never felt his absence so acutely. Never had to walk across the stage without his anchoring presence. Never had to address our company—our family of thousands of staff and consultants—

without him. There was no one to hold me up; no one who had "been there" to offer a shoulder, and no one who could authentically relate to my feelings of going from daughter and employee—to leader.

Standing backstage at The Bee, I listened as others moved through the program of scheduled events. Knowing my time to speak was quickly approaching, I felt my hands get clammy, fingertips turning to ice. I swallowed hard, not wanting to leave the protection found behind the curtain. I did not want to walk out there and stand in my Dad's place. I did not want to occupy the same square of platform or pretend to be excited about this turn of events. *As his daughter,* I did not want to do it. Because standing where he stood meant, in the most literal way, that *he was not there.* Standing where he stood meant that *everything was up to me.* Everyone here was depending on *me.*

I honestly didn't know if I could do it. Regardless of what my Dad had always taught me about courage, I can recall thinking on that day that my well did not run deeply enough to overcome such ever-present grief and abiding loss. I truly felt that the day my Dad died, my centering force died with him.

When my name was called, I swallowed the tears that were creeping up my throat and pushed the curtain aside. My feet seemed to walk forward without mental command, taking me to a place beyond my control or desire. But the clicking of heels on wood was quickly and authoritatively drowned out by the mass of humanity clapping for me from their seats.

One by one, our sales force stood up. They rose to their feet and thundered an ovation that completely overcame my sensibilities. I lifted my head to meet their outpouring of love and affirmation. They clapped and clapped and clapped—and I felt so . . . small. While I was entirely grateful for their support, there was certainly a level of discomfort in the adulation at the same time. All I could think of was that it should have been Dad. I was not ready for this. Because what they were saying during those long minutes of clapping and celebration was *"You are our leader. We are behind you! You can do it! We trust you!"*

The visual of this wide sea of believing people *depending on me* was overwhelming. And that's when I realized it: *Leading is not the same as managing. These people need more from me. They need a visionary and someone who can lead this company into the next chapter of its story. And Holy Cow—that someone is ME.*

As I worked over the next several years, part of me felt like I was working for a ghost; that although this company was now mine technically, I still felt the presence of my Dad everywhere. I still thought to myself *every day: What would Dad do?* He was so interwoven into everything we did, everything about me, everything about the company—how could I not? Success in those years was completely emotionally driven. I still wanted to make Dad proud. I still wanted to "prove" myself. I felt I had to.

But as I found my courage—and myself—in the midst of the changes, I discovered the truth in what my Dad had always told me: that the only strength you can find is from within. That it starts with self-acceptance. And with self-acceptance comes honesty, and a truer and fuller understanding of your limits.

I needed to grasp hold of that again—to find my courage to walk out on that stage and fill a pair of shoes that I never wanted to see empty. I needed to find the strength to begin to run Longaberger from *my vantage point*—not from the vantage point of a legacy. And I still need to find it every day. I need it to analyze numbers and determine the path forward, to deal with layoffs in a small town; to say good-bye to someone on Monday and have to see him at the grocery store on Tuesday.

In so many ways and so many situations, I have had to remind myself to find my courage. It's a daily choice—and a daily necessity.

Because finding courage is the first step to overcoming the fear in your mind. And I've learned that once you overcome the fear in your mind, *you can do anything.*

28 Grace in the Trying

Finding Courage in Difficult Circumstances

Sitting in my office at night, I was alone save for the steady clicking of the keyboard and my cell phone lighting up with new text messages from my kids asking where I was. I could hear the low hum of a vacuum rising and falling with each push off in the distance. A bookshelf behind me housed a pictorial exhibit of my life on paper: smiles suspended, black-and-white and living color, edges wrinkled, torn, repaired.

I leaned back in my chair, spinning to look past the photos and out the window, and thought of my Dad, and then of our Basketmakers. In my mind I saw each face I had known since childhood, pieced together family trees in the forest of my imagination.

I went to school with his son; shared the bleachers at a football game with her daughter; introduced him to my own children.

The only bittersweet crumb of working in a company that feels like family is that it *is* family. It's *personal*. And unfortunately, the recession of those years sprinted through America like a rabid dog that could care less about family—or layoffs.

But *I* did. And I still do.

Raking tired fingers through my hair, I contemplated the inevitable and fought against the gathering tide of doubt, battling unseen warriors within myself. *Could I figure out a way around this?* I wondered. *Maybe we could put it off for a few months—at least until after Christmas. . . . He just bought a new bass boat. Shoot. How are we going to tell him that we just can't keep his position anymore?*

Spreadsheet numbers blinked at me cruelly. I stared back, mind blank, looking at some imaginary space behind the screen until my vision went blurry. Breathing deeply, I tried to tell myself that it would be all right. That we'd get through it. But in my heart—in my gut—I knew it wasn't so simple; that it would never be totally cut-and-dried. I buried my head in my hands and felt the slow tremor of shoulders shaking. And I prayed that morning would never come.

Trying to explain the heaviness of those moments is like trying to describe the essence of a fragrance or color. You can make comparisons and draw illustrations, but how can the unknown truly become known until it's been experienced? By its very nature, this position is isolating and lonely. Aside from my father, there weren't many people I felt I could look to for guidance, empathy, or direction. And now that he's gone, I often feel absolutely and utterly alone—bearing the burden of guilt for those unmerciful spreadsheets and decisions that affect husbands and wives and college tuitions and bass boats, all by myself.

Walking onto the plant floor the next morning to talk to Bob,[*] I saw the face that I had known since high school. I thought of his kids and his recent divorce. I counted the number of years that he had been with the company.

---

[*] *Name has been changed*

Twenty.

Twenty years of bending splints and nailing copper hinges and proudly placing "Longaberger" tags on our products. And now I was supposed to let him go?

"Bob," I started, nearly choking on the words about to spew from my mouth. *"I wish there was someway around this. I wish it didn't have to be you. But in this tough economy . . . we need to make some cutbacks."*

He shifted his weight, examining the floor beneath his steel-toed boots and rubbing the back of his neck with calloused hands. When he finally looked up at me, he cleared his throat and breathed deeply.

"Bob, please believe me that if there were any other way. . . . " my voice trailed off as I tried to read his expression. I braced for the worst. *"We hope that in the next few months, if things pick up again, that we'll be able to bring you back. I really hope we can."*

"I understand, Tami. I do. We'll figure something out at home. Don't worry about us."

Don't worry? How could I not worry—about Bob and a thousand other Bobs who had become family to me?

I felt sick.

The tension in those moments is that I must convey compassion and regret and concern to one particular man or woman, yet in the next second—literally—I must turn around to face the rest of my Basketmakers and assure them that they still have a job! That the company is all right, that we're making necessary changes to survive for the long haul. Just as a vintner fastidiously prunes his grapes in season, painstakingly contemplating each snip that will lead to a healthier vineyard and better wine, the painful snips we make in Dresden will produce a stronger company.

Of course, I didn't really sign up to be a vintner, and sometimes I wonder if I really signed up for all of this heartache, either. On days like the ones when I have to talk to people like Bob about losing his job, I'm pretty sure I didn't.

Not too long ago I was out at the end of my driveway picking up trash that had collected along the margins of our county road. Most people in our small town know me and know where I live, so when the pickup truck that had just chugged past me stopped in the middle of the road, I didn't know what to expect.

Was this a disgruntled employee? A laid-off member of our Longaberger family? Nobody wants to think the worst, but in these times I suppose you just never know what people are capable of when bogged down in grief and feelings of rejection. It's not me or my home or possessions that I worry about; I worry about the safety of my kids.

The driver of the truck jockeyed it into reverse and slowly sent himself backward toward where I was, still picking up trash. I wasn't sure what to do. Lifting my head, I offered a weak wave, straining to recognize the face hiding under the low brim of a farm cap.

As he turned his head to face me, I recognized him. It was Tom. Tom had been with the company for years until we had to lay him off in the mid-2000s. My heart pinched and hiccupped, confined in an ever-tightening chest. I braced for a verbal onslaught—or worse.

Instead, true to his Ohio upbringing, Tom looked at me with eyes of kindly goodness; gentle, benevolent eyes that wished only the best for me and for Longaberger. *"Tami, I just wanted to tell you that I miss you. I miss being there with all you guys. And I pray every day for the company. I just wanted to stop and see how things are going."*

The knots in my stomach tightened their hold on my midsection, and I was sure my legs were sinking into the dirt. Instead of being salve for my wounds, Tom's kindness made me want to run and hide. I just felt so *responsible,* like I had let him — along with Bob and so many others—down. I realized that in our small town, there simply aren't a lot of options for employment and careers, and the fact that I was "pruning" the mainstay of Dresden made me feel awful about myself and about the decisions that had to be made.

Tom drove away, leaving me near the edge of the road with my bag of trash. I looked past the ghost of where he was and up to the brick façade of my house and instantly regretted building it. Even though half of it is used for company functions, at that moment it seemed a brazen expression of wealth in the face of loss. And I suddenly mourned the fact that my home was no longer a sanctuary. Instead, it became four walls surrounding me with a constant reminder of what I *had*—that so many others did not.

I don't share these things with you to garner sympathy, of course; I share them because we will all encounter struggles and trials at some point in our imperfect lives. And though our trials will be different, varied in stripe and duration, *we all must find it within ourselves to carry on.* We have to get out our scoops and shovels and *dig deep* in the well of courage every day. We have to have faith in each other.

And above all, we have to try to believe the best truth about our neighbor or friend, and try to exhibit grace in the trying.

Courage for the moment—and grace in the trying.

29 Horizon of Hope

Finding Courage in Illness

It's interesting to sit and watch kindergartners draw rainbows. With tongues wagging and brows furrowed, they tenderly pull waxy crayons from their boxed home, scribbling a rainbow of color with purpose. The product is generally a basic band of colors inspired by the prettiest of Crayola's practical eight-pack.

It must be said, however, that the world that we live in today comprises so many more shades of light. The prism now available to artists and non-artists alike provides seemingly endless color choices, where the slightest tone variation is deemed worthy of acquiring a new identity. Crayola has been whimsical and imaginative with its latest names; I find the following particularly fascinating:

Macaroni and Cheese

Fuzzy Wuzzy Brown

Jazzberry Jam

Wild Blue Yonder

Purple Mountains' Majesty

But as much as I appreciate the creativity and kid-friendly humor, in my estimation there is one color that needs no embellishment, no elaboration.

PINK.

Over the last 15 years, one look at this word conjures up a buffet of thoughts, connections, and reference points. For me and many others like me, *pink* equals Breast Cancer Awareness.

Having lived through a scary misdiagnosis myself in 2003, I can attest to the jolt of worry and perspective that comes with hearing the word *cancer*. Though I was spared from any serious health concerns, I understand the mental shuffling of years to come, imagining key events being played out when you're no longer there:

A daughter's wedding

That trip you've been wanting (and waiting) to take

The house you're saving up to buy

The degree you had always meant to get

A son's graduation

Checking off every last thing on your "Bucket List"

The birth of grandchildren

Seeing future calendar dates roll past your mind's eye like a spinning Rolodex is a dizzying experience. And for even the strongest among us, it becomes easy to break down, collapsing in despair and hopelessness.

But we at Longaberger know, and I know, that the best tool in anyone's cancer-fighting arsenal is *hope*. You simply cannot overestimate the reality of what hope can do for a warrior fighting off terrible news, new rounds of tests, more pricks and prods, and that ever-present spinning Rolodex. And with hope comes courage: the courage to fight, and the courage to overcome. And that's why Longaberger—in conjunction with the American Cancer Society—created the *Horizon of Hope* campaign in 1995.

Our goal is simple: To inform and educate women about the disease, while raising money for the American Cancer Society. Each year we design a limited line of *Hope* baskets and other home accessories that we offer through our Home Consultants, who remain ever-dedicated and contribute a portion of each sale to ACS. I am so proud to say that in a decade and a half, we have reached an estimated 20 million women with life-saving information and donated over $14 million for cancer research. It's amazing what a little *pink* will do!

Taking part in such a life-giving campaign has never been so meaningful as the summer I met Tina Marie Kennis. At that time, Tina was a new Branch Leader who had been invited to my home for lunch to celebrate her accomplishments in that role. We were all excited for her, and Tina's own feelings of personal satisfaction were evident.

Tina shared a little about her life and family during our luncheon, and I could see that she was a special woman. She had a husband and infant son waiting for her at home in New Jersey, and she loved the opportunity that Longaberger had given her to earn some extra money while keeping her personal priorities in line. In the course of our conversation, Tina made an offhanded comment about how earlier *that week* she had had a cyst removed from her breast. She had detected the lump while breast-feeding and was assured it was little more than a nuisance.

Unfortunately, upon arriving home and returning to the doctor to have the biopsy sutures removed, she was told that abnormal cells were found—and that in fact, she had a rare and aggressive form of breast cancer.

She was 29 years old. And she was newly pregnant.

Stunned and in complete disbelief, Tina raced home to process the news with her husband. What would this mean? How would they battle it? What kind of treatment was available? What about the baby?

Though clearly difficult and life-changing at *any* age, dealing with breast cancer at 29 seemed especially unthinkable. With so many questions looming, Tina and her husband decided to find the most reputable doctors available to them and seek their guidance and opinions.

Sadly, all of them agreed: Her cancer was rapidly growing and fueled by the fact that her pregnant body's estrogen levels were 1,000 times the normal amount. To avoid treatment meant to continue to feed the cancer; but to treat the cancer meant injecting her body—and thereby her unborn baby—with a deluge of toxic poisons delivering unknown consequences. Of the six doctors consulted, five concluded the worst; Tina would have to choose: her baby or her life.

Tina sobbed, annihilated with grief and heartbreak. To her, considering the termination of a planned and wanted pregnancy was worse than news of cancer itself. Yet to keep the baby and put her own life in jeopardy meant gambling on the life of her son's mother. The thought of orphaning her only child, then just one year old, seemed unconscionable. It was, in so many ways, a lose-lose proposition. So Tina decided there was no good choice—only a necessary one.

With her husband's support, they proceeded with the termination, hearts crushed, cancer breathing its ugly breath on their futures. She began chemotherapy and embarked on the journey that no one wants to take: nausea, weakness, hair loss, *fighting for her life.*

But in those moments, Tina embraced hope; and in doing so, found *courage*—the courage she needed to carry on. The courage she clung to in her darkest moments of personal struggle and loss. The courage to reach out to others in the midst of her own profound physical and emotional suffering.

You see, right in the middle of Tina's world crumbling, another was being woven together, splint by splint, hinge by hinge. We were days into our eighth year of *Horizon of Hope,* and Tina decided that there was no one better equipped to share the message of hope and courage than Tina herself.

And so, with eyelashes becoming more and more sparse, Tina opened her Longaberger business calendar. With eyebrows slipping away, she scheduled home parties so she could showcase the *Hope* baskets and tell others her story. With hair falling around her feet in the bathroom, she practiced what she wanted to say—what she wanted others to hear. And with a bald head, she went out night after night to raise cancer awareness, showcasing baskets with a flair of pink, an infamous twisted ribbon, a pamphlet tucked inside. Tina now says that *Horizon of Hope* gave her strength—the kind of strength that comes from drawing upon and contributing to something larger than yourself.

Tina embodied *hope.* She embodied *courage.*

And with the tide of courage lifting her further onto the shores of hope, Tina took her efforts one step further by creating her own local event she dubbed *In the Pink.* Working in tandem with area businesses and vendors, Tina and her team of Longaberger consultants organized a women's luncheon in her town—and her efforts were truly inspiring.

Tina didn't stop there, though. She went on to work with the governor of New Jersey to create a bill that would force health insurance companies to provide mammograms to women of any age, and was privileged to be at his side when the bill was signed into law. She has continued to help other consultants replicate her *In the Pink* luncheons all over the country, providing hope and courage to hundreds.

And all the while, through days of treatment and nights of agony and private suffering, Tina found strength in the endless support she received from her Longaberger family. It wasn't just my phone calls that gave her a boost; it was, as she tells it, the daily trip to her mailbox that sent her reeling. Amazingly, Tina received notes and cards and letters from all over the United States, from other consultants who had heard her story and were touched deeply by it. Flowers sent by another who wished her well and was praying for her.

She was surrounded by the kind of support that keeps your spirit afloat in the storm; the kind of love that anchors your person and your heart.

In 2006, I was honored to invite her back to share her story at my home for an audience of 150 people. After concluding her story of cancer and finding strength and purpose in the *Horizon of Hope* campaign, she stood for a moment at the podium. She breathed deeply, exhaled.

"It has been a long, slow struggle to return to health. I've had to wade through seemingly endless deep waters without sure footing; been forced to decide the impossible: to return my beloved unborn baby to God. These years have been the most difficult ones I've ever been through. But I stand here today and rejoice to tell you that—despite doctors' concerns to the contrary—*I am pregnant again.*"

Pregnant! What an announcement for Tina to make—and what a joy to hear it in my own home! We all clapped with the kind of vigor that comes from love and concern and true celebration. It was a remarkable, wonderful moment.

Tina is an amazing woman who grasped onto hope and found the courage to overcome horrible and potentially paralyzing health issues. She reached deep within amid a moment of trial and surpassed all expectations. She is a truly exemplary model for the rest of us to follow.

Why do I share her story? Why not talk about something more palatable—like the courage of a young consultant starting her business against all odds? Or a brave friend who dashed through fiery walls to save the family dog? Why choose a story about cancer?

Because, in short, I believe that there are far too many Tinas in this world; far too many women and men whose lives are cut short or compromised while the rest of the world goes about their daily business. And I firmly believe that we must work together to turn this around! And I'm proud that Longaberger is taking steps, however large or small, in the direction of *hope.*

So the next time you reach for a box of crayons and pull out a pink, think of Tina. Think of Tina and the millions of other women who battle this faceless disease. And consider what you might do to begin to make a difference in the fight.

Maybe it's organizing a fundraising luncheon or a golf outing, or partnering with a movement like *Horizon of Hope.* Or maybe it's something small but priceless, like buying a scarf for your friend whose hair is succumbing to the rigors of chemo, or sitting with her at the doctor's office or sharing a cup of tea in her living room. Maybe it's buying a basket in her honor to support our Horizon of Hope Campaign.

It is as simple as including some pink in your rainbow while remembering that no matter what you call it, it's hope for someone like Tina.

And keeping in mind that whatever the source—hope brings courage for us all.

Part 8
Sharing and Giving Back

30 Hands in Dresden Dirt

My Love for Nature and the Beauty of the Earth

When winter snows begin their slow regression back into the earth, making way for tulip buds and new growth on maples, something primal deep within me begins to stir and itch. I yearn to get outside under the yellow May sunshine and plunge my hands into the dirt around my home. I wait all winter to experience the cool, damp earth on my fingers and under my nails—to inhale the heady organic smell of soil that is like nothing else in this world.

The time I spend in the garden and on forest pathways are moments of rebirth and renewal for me. Away from phones and calendars and appointments, I am absolutely calm. Absolutely refreshed. Absolutely myself.

Nobody needs anything from me. No one plops manila folders in my lap or spreadsheets on my desk. Nobody asks for a press release or a meeting time. I do not have to produce anything earth-shattering or life altering; I do not have to create. There are no decisions to be made in a garden; I can just *be*.

And to me, that is precious. Because what the earth shares with me is life itself.

Spending a few hours in the natural world helps me to feel centered and grounded. The strains that come from a bad economy or unavoidable layoffs, though always present, begin to fade into the dusk of evening. The sloping sun bleeds through a nearby stand of trees, calling out to the deer and great blue herons, the kingfishers and beavers. Leaving the safety of the forest and the reeds at water's edge, they emerge wide-eyed and beautiful. And I stand as a witness to their grace, gaining perspective on the day and appreciation for those small moments of fresh air and dreamy haze.

It is, most certainly, my truest sanctuary.

Experiencing this kind of intimate exchange with our amazing planet has been special to me since I was a little girl, skipping through summer in Dresden. I can still remember spending hours upon hours out in my Grandma Eschman's sprawling garden, poking holes into rows of dirt, preparing the way for seeds that held the promise of new life in minuscule encapsulated bodies. With tiny hands browning in the heat of midday, I would work alongside my mother, sister, and grandparents to bury those seeds, water them, and then wait with patient expectation for the promise of sprouts new and green.

Tending this garden was where it all started for me, though I suppose some would claim that it's simply in my blood. With pride in their heritage, my mother's extended Eschman family can still be found farming the same patch of German countryside that has belonged to us *since 1574*. Through years of joy and hardship, we've remained there; agrarian and hardworking, tilling and churning and cultivating the land that has both provided for them in good times and stripped them of everything they had in leaner years.

As if carrying the torch in her own small way here in the United States, my mother was a member of our local garden club in Dresden. And though her efforts were never pretentious or fancy, she swelled to bring freshly cut flowers into our home. A piece of the outdoors brought in to cast an explosion of color across the room of our modest abode; it was God's artwork in its truest form.

In the fall, Rachel and I would traipse over uneven ground with rickety old wheelbarrows to bring in the harvest of gourds. Working with care, we would let them dry in the late September sunshine before hollowing them into birdhouses. Simple and unique in form, we were jubilant when the purple martins, swallows, and chickadees poked around and resolved to take up residence inside our architectural debuts.

Even now, so many years later, you'll still find me at home with a pair of binoculars in one hand and McCormac & Kennedy's *Birds of Ohio* in the other. Of the 400 or so birds that can be seen in my home state, I've been fortunate to have spotted over 100 on my property alone. As they flit across my fields and meander through surrounding meadows, it is not only their delicate little bodies that take flight; it's my heart as well.

One of the most rewarding parts of motherhood for me—in addition, of course, to raising wonderful, kind people who are productive members of society—has been teaching and instilling a love for nature within my children, Claire and Matthew. When the kids were little, we began traveling and exploring the treasures of our country's national parks. As trips came more frequently and the kids grew to adore the creativity and beauty of land undisturbed by human hands, Matt conjured up a goal that we took on as a family: to visit all of our national parks during his lifetime.

It didn't take very long during our first visit to Yellowstone to fall completely in love with the majesty of its wild places. I stood at the foot of the Rockies and imagined all the lives that have come and gone, over time, passing through those same shadows. I saw buffalo breathe and snort the fog of early morning. I watched the way a mama black bear tumbled down an embankment with her cub and absorbed the utter splendor of centuries-old trees. And through all of this, I sensed the hand of something so much bigger at work.

On one particularly poignant morning, I decided to get up early and hike to a nearby peak in time to take in the sunrise alone. As I reached the top of the lookout, I found a snatch of ground to sit on and wait for the show—and what a show it was! A low morning sun gained momentum and spilled over the top of the adjacent eastern ridge, pouring into the valley below and filling the sky with gold and amber and yellow. Behind me, the snow on the western slopes glowed pink in the light of dawn.

The majesty was breathtaking; so much so that I felt my eyes sting with tears. I knew that the gift of this morning was being shared with me in the most intimate and emotional of ways, as though I was learning words to a new, unspoken language; reciting a mysterious melody like a cantor in God's own church. It was amazing, and incredibly spiritually moving.

Our trips since that time have taken us to the deserts of Sedona, to Montana's Glacier National Park, the Grand Tetons of Wyoming, Acadia National Park in Maine—and countless others. And at each place, I felt the earth sharing life with me.

So how could I not wish to share that life with others?

In the early 2000s, when my home, Eschman Meadows, was built on 250 acres, I knew that one of my non-negotiables would be to preserve and reinstate as much of the wilderness around me as possible. I worked excitedly with local experts and friends to return 40 of those acres to native Ohio prairies. They taught me about the kinds of trees, grasses, flowers, and plants that I would need to bring in to achieve this goal. They showed me photos of the kinds of animals I could expect to reappear after their long-destroyed habitat had been restored. They helped me to understand what it would take to maintain this dream of mine—and why it was so very worth it.

I often have the opportunity to invite Longaberger employees, consultants, and loyal customers into my home for lunch or other company events. We celebrate together, share in each other's triumphs, and enjoy conversation over a plate of wonderful food. One of the highlights of those days for me, aside from meeting each member of our extended family, is sharing my home—my little world that so refreshes me and plugs me in to life on a bigger scale. Seeing consultants roam my grounds freely, taking in the earth as nature intended it, gives me great joy. I love sharing that with them.

Standing beside my children through the years as they grew to appreciate our land—while listening to their dreams of seeing the best our world has to offer—has always made me grateful. I loved seeing their young faces light up when they saw their first bison or drank up their first sunset at the ocean. I'm so blessed to have helped instill in them a love for the natural, physical world around them.

Sitting alone in my garden or atop a mountain peak, I am thankful for small moments; whispers that speak to my soul at dawn and remind me of my place in this world. Those moments help to realign my perspective—help to recall the scale and brevity of our lives—yours and mine.

I am grateful that simply by virtue of our humanity, we are invited to share in the gorgeous landscape of our world; a landscape that is mysterious and ancient, constantly changing and timeless. I am indebted to the earth for what it's taught me, for the ways in which it speaks to me, and for all that it shares with me.

And mostly, I am grateful for the Dresden dirt that I call home.

31 Random Acts of Kindness

Teaching My Children the Joy of Giving

The rain had been coming down in sheets all week, and this first break in the clouds sent our family bursting into the expanse of our front yard, yearning for the fresh smell of spring that follows rain. As we wandered the winding road that led to my barn, Claire and I stopped to investigate the myriad of potholes that had morphed into tiny ponds, perfect for frogs to lay eggs and spawn their young.

Amazed at these critters' resourcefulness, my mind spun forward in time and realized that once the sun came out, they wouldn't be so lucky. Their corner on the real estate market was about to dry up, and that spelled T-R-O-U-B-L-E for their little ones. Gathering buckets and filling them from a nearby pond, we set out on a small relocation project.

"Okay, now be careful, Claire," I warned my daughter, who was just a little girl at the time. "We have to scoop them *all* up; we can't leave any behind." I watched as her small hands dove deep into the craters of our dirt road, craters filled with tiny black tails whipping furiously, sleek bodies cutting through murky water.

I helped her catch each one, quickly and with care, and then send them flapping into our buckets. Up and down the gravel road we moved, looking for life in each pothole, and then releasing them into our pond.

When my friend saw us hard at work with the diligence of firemen in a burning building, she stopped and said, "Tami, why are you doing that? What difference is it going to make?"

I looked at her and then turned my gaze to the bucket hanging from my dirty fingers. "It'll make a difference to these tadpoles."

That moment—that one small activity in our own front yard—began to inform my children's understanding of kindness and giving. Because giving of our time, for those tadpoles, meant *giving life.*

I've always loved animals and nature, and I've raised Claire to grow up loving the same things. It's been so gratifying to see her stop to rescue an animal on the side of the road or nurse a bird with a broken wing. Showing kindness to an animal, I believe, is the budding beginning of a gracious, loving, and giving heart.

Recently, I was on a bike ride with my friend Madge. It was a gorgeous day and we decided to tackle a short eight-mile trail near our homes. Riding under the canopy of fresh buds and flowering trees was oxygen for my soul. I breathed in the freshness of April, memorizing the rocks and dirt and sprouts of life on the margins of our path.

As we approached our turn-around point, I saw her. Sitting still in the center of the trail, a silhouette against the backdrop of forest, was a cat. We were in the middle of nowhere! I knew this cat was lost or homeless, and when I see a stray cat, it's a done deal. There are no adoption papers or declarations; that cat will inevitably be coming home with me.

And thus, I rode the last four miles with one hand steering my bike, a ball of fur and love in the other.

It's always been my earnest desire to display this kind of love in my life every day—because kids *see what you do* far more often than they hear what you say. I've learned that the most effective parenting strategy is to *demonstrate* what I want them to do, rather than just *tell* them what to do.

This translates for us financially as well, as I'm sure it does for many of you. Whether you donate canned goods to your local food bank or mittens to the Angel Tree, showing kindness when you don't know the recipient and won't see their joy is a powerful lesson for kids. It's easy to give when it's someone you love; it's gratifying to do so when you're there for the elation and screams of surprise. But when you're removed and you give *just to give,* without any expectation of something tangible or intangible in return—*that* is a wonderful thing.

When Claire and Matt were younger, I remember driving into the grocery store parking lot and seeing a raggedy man standing near the curb holding a ratty sign: "Will Work For Food."

I reached for my wallet and decided to spread some sunshine on what appeared to be a dreary day in his world. Handing him a $20 bill, my kids and I watched in shock as he examined it, stuffed it in his stained pant pocket, rolled up his sign, and went home. I guess that was all he needed!

I laugh about it now, considering all the things my $20 may have gone to support. But I leave those thoughts on the doorstep of my heart, recognizing that I gave just to give; just because I wanted to, with no strings attached. No motive or hopes for something in return. And in doing so, I could not look at that $20 as though it were still mine, wondering and pressing for answers and explanations. My gift—my random act of kindness—became *his.*

Over the years, my children have made friends with kids who came from homes that struggled a little more than others. Befriending them because of who they were—as people and unique individuals—was my kids' choice. Sharing with them and giving out of love was a choice *I made* so that my children could witness it.

A handful of Matt's friends used to come to our house and stay for the weekend. We would share meals and eat breakfast together, the boys playing all afternoon and well into the evening. They became part of our extended family, and in a way, like surrogate sons of my own.

As Matt became more active in sports and signed up for basketball camps, we'd discuss plans in the kitchen and watch as his friends stared at their feet, avoiding eye contact during our conversations. It became obvious that they wouldn't be going to basketball camp.

"Listen," I told several of them privately, " . . . if you keep your grades up and stay eligible, I'll pay for your basketball camp."

Their eyes lit up, considering the possibilities, and they did it! And so did the others. Like a proud mother, I'm happy to say that two of those kids have gone on to college with partial sports scholarships. While I, of course, don't take the credit for that, it gives me great joy to be counted among the links in the chain of their story. Nowadays, we cheer those boys on by clipping their articles out of the paper and adding them to our "Wall of Fame" in the kitchen. We watch them and read about them and send them encouraging cards and text messages. Cutting articles and sending notes is a tangible way that we love those boys and continue to hold them up, supporting them through the rigors of college and life.

Another thing I've been intentional about teaching my children is to give generously and freely to those working in the service industry—and to treat them with respect. Whether it's tipping a doorman, speaking to the housekeeper, or showing kindness to a receptionist, it's a priority that I don't take lightly.

In my estimation, how a person behaves *when they think it doesn't matter* is of grave importance. People are people, and people *everywhere* deserve to be treated with unequivocal respect. If my children can't learn to show love and kindness and grace to *everyone,* then their ability to treat prominent individuals with kindness doesn't matter. That may seem easy or obvious, but I assure you, it's not. I've seen the underside of this too many times to let it slide off my back.

Ask yourself how you're doing in this area. When was the last time you put a card in the mail to encourage a friend, or baked cookies for your neighbor? How often are you willing to part with a couple of dollars when it comes to a charity or cause that's important to you? Do you model exemplary kindness and respect when you talk to the men and women checking your bags at the airport? Clearing the table at your favorite restaurant? Polishing your nails at the salon? You may think those interactions don't really matter—but they do.

Your actions are an outpouring of your heart, and your heart becomes visible in each of those moments. Make sure the heart you're revealing is one of love and kindness.

32 Come Along with Me

Sharing My Days with Others

Though Alex Shumate served with me on The Ohio State University Board of Trustees, he is perhaps better known for his role as Global Managing Partner of Squire, Sanders, and Dempsey Law Firm. Several years ago, as we discussed the university's projects and financial needs, he told me about a popular saying he once heard at church: that when it comes to giving, you can choose to offer up your time, talent, or treasure.

One click of the remote control confirms what Alex taught me that day; we are people who reach out and give in a variety of ways, both tangibly and intangibly. With warnings of floods or other natural disasters, we witness volunteers lobbing sand bags and hammering windows shut in pounding rain. They labor around the clock to protect the towns and cities they love from the threat of storms and perilous weather. In similar fashion, schools and churches rushed to ship clothes, medical supplies, and food to Haiti in the wake of this year's devastating earthquake.

The Internet sounds off about neighborhoods coming together to help a friend keep their home, buying it back from the bank, effectively pulling it out of the pit of foreclosure and rescuing their neighbors from homelessness. Folks come out in force to serve Thanksgiving dinner to those spending the holiday in shelters across the country. Our world gives us a plethora of concrete examples, demonstrating what it looks like to give back, to share with others, and pay it forward.

The truth is that in this economy in particular, families feel pinched to meet their household budget, making it nearly impossible to give additional financial gifts. Instead, these individuals take stock of their skills and talents, seeking an alternative to the expected. Some dust off their tools and contribute a hard day of measuring, sawing, and nailing to Habitat for Humanity. Others may make a meal for a family coping with postoperative complications or spend the afternoon mowing the lawn for an older gentleman next door.

On the other hand, folks with financial resources are often fairly busy. They live frenetic lives with multiple commitments scratched in their planners, all pressing for their time and attention. To them, giving is easiest done by getting out a checkbook and donating money. They feel gratified to remain connected to the work of the organization while still experiencing the joy of sharing.

All of these acts of kindness and sharing are helpful—and *necessary*—in our world. And wherever you fall on the spectrum of giving time, talent, or treasure, you should be encouraged that your participation is making a difference. All three add the kind of warmth and thankfulness reminiscent of the front porch neighborhoods of our parents and grandparents. Each act of human touch and interaction is a blessing to the recipient.

I feel especially lucky that I have been able to give in all three of those ways at some point in my life. But most meaningful to me is being able to throw wide the doors of Longaberger to young people seeking to gain new skills and improve themselves by expanding their knowledge. Nothing gives me greater joy than coming alongside someone and sharing my day with them—providing them with a peek inside corporate life and allowing them a window into a future that is theirs for the taking.

I certainly could not talk about sharing my days without telling the story of my summer with a young woman named Allison Streuter. She is a shining star in my night sky, and I hold her up as an example of what people can do if they truly invest their whole hearts.

Allison grew up watching her mother, Cathy O'Connell, build a life around her Longaberger business. Standing in the shadows as her parents' marriage dissolved, Allison watched Cathy plunge herself into work, maintaining a full-time job outside of the home and making connections for Longaberger at night.

Allison saw firsthand that Longaberger was a positive force in her mother's life. It provided for them financially while building Cathy's self-confidence and helping her regain lost independence. As Allison tells it, being a member of the Longaberger community was *family* to them. It got her mother through the pain of divorce and gave her the kind of hope she needed to find a glimmering path to the future.

As Cathy grew in her business and rose up in the company, she was able to quit her day job and focus solely on Longaberger. Her growing success led her to attend more and more sales events, giving me the opportunity to get to know both Cathy and Allison. Then in late May 2008, as Cathy prepared to lead a sales meeting in Schaumburg, Illinois, I called to ask if she'd mind if I stopped in and joined them. She was thrilled!

Walking into the banquet room, I was immediately impressed. Name tags, folders, and handouts were neatly organized at the check-in table. Guest tables were dressed in smooth tablecloths and bedecked with centerpieces that were simple but pretty. Chairs were pushed in, microphones were being checked—and all of this was handled in swift fashion by Allison.

With the dew of graduation still fresh upon her, Allison soaked up the moments she could spend with her mother, assisting in Cathy's efforts to train and motivate the men and women now comprising her expanding sales team. Flitting around the room wrapping up loose ends, Allison spotted me out of the corner of her eye and quickly made her way across the room. Tucking long hair behind her ears, she extended her hand and thanked me for coming, noting how very much it meant to her mother and what a joy it was to her personally.

"It's always good to see you, Allison," I said, offering a hug. "So, you're helping your mom with this event?"

"Yeah," she answered, "I just graduated from the University of Iowa and am back at home now, so I'm happy to help."

"So what's the next step? What will you be doing this summer?"

"Looking for a job!" she smiled. "I'd love to find something in event planning."

"You would be perfectly suited for that! Wouldn't it be great if you could come work for Longaberger this summer? Maybe you could come help with The Bee." Allison looked hopeful, and I made mental note to follow up with her when I returned to Ohio.

We had never taken on interns for The Bee, but I knew we needed help—and I was certain that Allison was the woman for the job. More importantly, providing opportunities to teach others and learn in a practical, hands-on environment is something of utmost importance to me. I was determined to make sure that she made it to Newark, Ohio, that summer, so I created the position just for her.

Starting on June 16, 2008, Allison moved into the local Longaberger-owned hotel and was immediately thrust into the realities of event planning. She began looking for props, ordering teaching materials, decorating sets, designing and photographing displays, and running all over Central Ohio with the tasks of Bee preparation. Over the next six weeks, she gained experience building up and tearing down sets, numbering and color coordinating, and keeping track of minuscule details. She would disassemble displays, bubble wrap and pack everything, and ensure that it all made it on the truck to Columbus for the big event. While at The Bee, Allison was hustling backstage, handling the hundreds of prizes and gifts awarded to consultants each year. It was no small undertaking!

At the end of July, with The Bee successfully behind her, Allison wrapped up the internship and returned home to begin searching earnestly for a permanent job. She returned, briefly, to the independent concert promoter she had worked with over the years, yearning to find employment in the entertainment industry. After interviews came up empty, Allison decided to take a couple weeks to visit a friend in Los Angeles.

As fate would have it, her friend worked at a talent agency that had an opening, and she urged Allison to apply. On a whim she rolled the dice, submitted her resume, interviewed while in the city, and returned home to wait to Illinois for the news.

Only the news didn't come.

Disappointed but not despairing, the setback shed light on Allison's desire to work in the music industry, deeming it a better fit for her creative bent. She talked it over with her mom and realized that to fully pursue this dream, she would have to move. In a courageous step of risking it all and believing in herself, Allison bravely gambled everything: She left home and family and friends to follow her heart.

Cathy looked at her little girl, now all grown up and preparing to move cross-country, and felt the stinging, melting kind of love that a mother feels when apron strings are untied. Yet when she saw the hope in Allison's eyes, she knew she would support her completely. That day, Cathy started the process of letting go, helping to pack her daughter's life into the back of a car. Years and days and memories—all stuffed into boxes on their way to the West Coast.

With windows down and warm air promising summer and happiness, Allison barreled across the Plains with her mom and grandmother at her side as traveling companions. Suddenly, she looked down to see the lights flashing on her phone, ringer drowned out by sounds of the highway: It was the talent agency she had interviewed with nearly two weeks earlier. Frantically rolling up the window to take the call, she was elated to hear that they were offering her the job! Her step of faith was answered with applause. On a Saturday in the middle of Nebraska, Allison prepared to start her new life.

Allison has worked tirelessly in the time since, garnering the attention of her superiors, earning promotions and successive interviews for other prestigious job openings. After a year and a half of inching closer to her goals, Allison landed her dream job as an assistant to a music manager—and is now touring with an international recording artist! When I last talked to her, she had just returned from Tokyo and was enjoying a brief respite before jetting off to Europe.

Allison is quick to thank me and—through tears—credit me with her success, saying that I helped her more fully believe in herself. But just as quickly, I turn the mirror around to show her the true source of her strength: *herself.*

I am proud to have opened doors for this remarkable young woman, to have given her a window of purpose and room to dream. I find great joy in giving of my time and talent so that others may discover their own. However, credit is also due her *own mother*—the woman who ignited small sparks and modeled strength and perseverance for her daughter, year after year. It is the layering of many days made up of small moments that solidified Allison's desire to achieve her goals.

Her recent e-mail is a beautiful testament to strong, determined women everywhere, especially working moms who wonder about the futures of their daughters. If you are one of those women—one of those moms—take note. You might be getting a letter like this someday yourself.

> Dear Tami,
>
> . . . I would not be here today if it were not for the inspiration and opportunity you have given my mother and myself. I learned so much from growing up and watching my mom grow her Longaberger business into what it is today, and watching her do something she is so passionate about. Having a mom that is strong, hardworking, passionate, and independent made me want to become that as well. Thank you, Tami, for instilling passion into the lives of so many.
>
> Love,
>
> Allie

How can you influence a young woman in your own life? What talents, skills, and areas of giftedness could you be sharing right now? Don't diminish your worth and the value of what only *you* can offer the world. Rise up and join a young woman on her journey.

You may never know the depth and breadth of your influence; you may never get to see her putting it all on the line to follow her heart. You may never get to witness her receiving the answers to a thousand different wishes and prayers.

But you truly never know.

Maybe, after loving another, the wishes and prayers that will be answered *will be your own.*

33 Landing in the Desert

Sharing Business with the Women of the Middle East

Looking out the compact airplane window to the ground below, all I could see was sand. Like an expansive capsule of brown stretched from north to south and east to west, only miniature-looking cinder-block buildings and national flags punctuated the terrain. Cars sped in rhythm below on streets reminiscent of the maple splints that fashion our baskets: long, lean, earthy. One question after another flashed in my mind, as—unbeknownst to me—I was embarking on a new adventure.

The sky allowed me only a partial snapshot of Jordan, a country I would come to love. In those early days, I beheld only a singular portion of the admiration and fondness that would grow in my heart. Now I've come to possess the whole: a heartfelt appreciation that's been carefully assembled in harmony by kindhearted people, delicious food, and the rich history of an ancient place. This connection is exceedingly precious to me, and as such, I choose to continue investing in its origin: The Middle East.

Two years ago, I was honored to receive a call from the White House inviting me to serve as chair on the Arab Women Leadership Institute—a Washington, D.C., based organization composed of nine women from Bahrain, Lebanon, Jordan, Iraq, Morocco, Palestine, and Tunisia. The goal of our efforts is to witness more women stepping forward as civil servants, female parliament members, and university students in their respective countries.

Our big-picture objective is to build an academy in the Middle East—most likely in Jordan—that would continue to partner with women who are making social advances in their countries. What I love about this idea is that it would *not* be U.S.-run, or even U.S.-led. When this academy is built, it will be owned and run by women from within the Middle East. *What a victory!*

My trips to the Middle East—mainly to Jordan—have been infused with wonder and intrigue. While I'm there—in the midst of ancient landscapes and languages—I ponder the civilizations that have gone before, that trod the same dirt now pounded flat beneath my feet. I think about the people who, through the ages, floated, suspended and weightless, in the same Dead Sea. I close my eyes and can clearly see robed men and women, cloaked and protected from searing sun, wandering over the same hills and through the same valleys I myself have just roamed. It's a truly remarkable thought.

I've said many times that if time could be flipped backward, manipulated for our mere convenience and delight, I would make myself a fresh-faced 20-year-old full of idealism and innocence. If—and only if—there was no Longaberger Company for me to return to after my college tenure at Ohio State University, I would pursue a degree in anthropology.

Of course, this is merely daydreaming; but the idea of cultures and their unique place on this globe is absolutely captivating to me. Imagine the many layers of history: Bricks and stone, clay jars

and ladles, tents and nomads, birthing stones and babies. Like the
thin skins of an onion demanding to be peeled away, these details
act as subtle velum on the stories of ancient globe-trotters.
Though they allow us to see more, to gather bits and pieces, we
still stretch in vain to gain the clarity we desire.

But it's more than speculations about archaeology or artifacts
for me. I wonder: Did the people of long ago relish hummus the
way I do? Did they slave for long hours on their delicious
tabbouleh, gathering fresh tomatoes and finely chopping parsley,
bulgur, and mint? Did their children beg for kibbeh the way I
would have? The fragrance of the cooking, the spices and
seasonings and fresh vegetables charm me.

The more deeply entrenched I become in this part of the
world, the more I realize how deeply I care for its people—in
particular, for its women. Working and interacting with Middle
Eastern women has broadened my thinking and challenged my
values. It has helped me to discover things that I never knew I
loved—and stirred them in until their individual components
dissolve away into the larger whole. It has cemented my belief that
we are not called to act as *moral judge* over another, but rather that
we should, as humans, value *all people*.

Helping these underrepresented women has also reminded me
of my own struggles, at times putting them into perspective. Many
of the women I meet are also working with family members and
feel an obligation to follow the direction charted by their fathers
or brothers. Many have dreams that must be carefully sheltered
and nurtured until they ripen, allowing them to be set free.

It gives me *such joy*—such *immense satisfaction*—to think that
something I might say or impress upon these women could turn a
key and unlock a door for them. In their endeavors to progress
socially, I feel privileged to walk beside them, helping them see
new paths and encouraging them as they negotiate unfamiliar

ground. I love to give of myself in this way; it is "paying it forward" in the best possible sense.

As I write on this lovely April morning, I reflect on another wonderful opportunity I recently had to sit down with a group of 15 young men and women from Lebanon, Jordan, and the United Arab Emirates. Sponsored by a grant through the U.S. State Department, the University of Toledo College of Business Administration orchestrated a meeting between me, several other Longaberger employees, and this inspiring group of traveling learners. The common thread sewn through us all—whether American or Middle Eastern—was that we are all working in family-owned businesses.

I began with a brief introduction of Longaberger's history, explained how basketmaking has been in our family for 100 years, and then opened our time up to questions. Many asked wonderfully insightful things like "How do you stay current?," "How can you compete with the Chinese who can make baskets faster and cheaper?," and "How did you handle the transition when your dad died?"

Spending time on each question and providing as much detail as possible, we began a truly collaborative dialogue. And just as I knew it would, that familiar feeling came creeping back in—the one that reminds me how we're all *so much more similar* than we are different.

These folks, believe it or not, were worried about working with *their* dads. They were worried about competitors and foreign markets. They wondered about branding and marketing and sales techniques. And they asked about all of the fantastic consultants who are out in the field, sharing our products with men and women all over the United States. They left wondering, "Could direct sales work in Lebanon? In Jordan? In the United Arab Emirates?"

Sharing my story as these people process and grow their own is a powerful catalyst for compassion and love and enthusiasm. It makes me passionate about Longaberger all over again, and excited about each person who commits daily to running his—or *her*—personal business. And most of all, it makes me thrilled to stretch the imaginations of people who, at their core, are just like me: who want the best for their employees; who stay up late trying to find a way to do the seemingly impossible; who are creative and innovative and relevant. They are people who love their families and want their family business to succeed; who are looking forward to a brighter tomorrow where we can all work together, helping and cheering, as part of a global family that Longaberger is committed to joining.

So tell me about your "desert." Do you have a place that sparks your imagination and broadens your thinking? Where is it?

As we move further into a new decade, perhaps you can ask yourself: What can I do to add some color to my life, to experience a new culture and open the doors of my mind a little bit wider? Am I the victim of too much "vanilla"? In other words—do I make an effort to expose myself to people with different worldviews, perspectives, religions, and lifestyles? And if I don't—why? Sometimes taking that first step outside of your comfort zone can be terribly difficult; many times, we *allow* fear to paralyze us.

So resolve to dig deep within yourself this year, and truly *believe* that developing an expanded lens on life has the power to sharpen and revitalize you. It will add color and texture and music to a life of homogeny.

Try to land in the desert this year.

And see where the road leads you. . . .

34 Philanthropy

A Way of Life

In 1997, shortly after my Dad was diagnosed with cancer, he sat down with Rachel and me and discussed how we could ensure that a portion of his abundant blessings would continue to enhance others' lives. It was vital to Dad that we would work with purpose and foresight to ensure that those in need—particularly those in our geographical area—would have the opportunity to better themselves and improve their quality of life. Since we had always witnessed our father modeling this approach in his life anyway, taking the next "official" step forward was a logical progression— one that propelled our family journey with a renewed forward momentum of benevolence.

And so, it was in the spirit of sharing and giving back that my father established The Longaberger Foundation. Over the years, we've continued to make contributions to fulfill commitments my father made long ago—commitments that encourage entrepreneurship, enhance local parks and recreation facilities, and enrich the educational opportunities for Ohio residents, to name a few. And it's been our joy during this time to see how small gestures can make way for big ripples of positive effects.

At the heart of our Foundation is a commitment to the betterment of our employees and their families; as such, the vast majority of our grants are awarded to organizations right here in southern Ohio where we live, work, and play. With recipients residing, for the most part, in Muskingum County and surrounding areas, we strive to continually invest in the lives of our workforce and our community.

If Dresden is the heartbeat of Longaberger, then the nation— and our consultants in each state—are the hands, feet, life, and limbs of our company. As a way of acknowledging our national sales force, we have thoughtfully chosen a cause that touches so many of our extended family members, either directly or indirectly. With funds raised exceeding $14 million, the Horizon of Hope Campaign is a partnership between our company, our consultants and the American Cancer Society, aimed at fighting breast cancer. I am so proud of the progress we've made to educate more than 20 million men and women about early detection, to fund important research, and furthermore, to aid them in leading healthy lives that will reduce their risks of developing breast cancer.

The Longaberger Foundation and Horizon of Hope aren't just changing lives *outside* our brick-and-mortar building. They're changing lives *inside,* too.

I can personally attest to the fact that it's made a difference in mine by giving me a fantastic opportunity to model giving in my own children's lives. My work on the foundation and with Horizon of Hope affords me moments to teach Claire and Matthew how to share financial resources in a formal way; allows me to walk next to them as they begin to ask questions and formulate opinions; and grants me opportunities to stretch their young minds in broader, more selfless directions.

To bring them more fully into this work of sharing, I recently added both Claire and Matthew to our foundation's board of directors. Because they're now both over the age of 18, it is a meaningful and participatory way for them to learn about the responsibility of charitable giving. Modeling this kind of proactive and planned philanthropy is very important to me.

As we undertake to steer this philanthropic ship, we've passed many who wave at us and testify to new beginnings. New chapters opened up—new stories of new days. Hearing these stories is one of the most gratifying parts of my job; it humbles me and fills me with thanks. These accounts are powerful reminders of how taking the time to listen, to ponder, and ultimately, to give, doesn't just change someone else's life; *it might just change your own.*

One of the first acts of giving that the foundation assumed was to set up a scholarship for women at Ohio State University. The Ohio State Critical Difference for Women Re-Entry Scholarship is aimed at supporting women who have had their education interrupted by life circumstances. Whether their journey included an unplanned pregnancy, a job loss, or a family emergency, the women who have benefited from this scholarship over the last decade have been given the gift of a new start. What's more, they've been given the chance to act as role models for a younger generation of women who have seen them overcome hurdles and arise victorious.

Aliza Finegold's father died when she was just 15 years old. Killed in a horrific train crash, he was suddenly gone, leaving Aliza's mother to raise her and four sisters on her own. In those days of grief and despair, Aliza's eyes were opened to the awful circumstances in which their family now found itself. Furthermore, it occurred to her that if her mother hadn't had a career in insurance sales, they would have been in *real* trouble. At 15, she *understood* the necessity for women to maintain their careers and choose to work in a field with good earning potential. She saw in her own home how it made the difference between thriving and surviving.

Aliza graduated from New York University's nursing school in 2001 and worked for a couple of years before having her first child with her husband, a business broker and rabbi. After the baby came, Aliza took some time off and prepared to help move their family to Ohio. It was then that she realized that she wanted to continue her education and earn her master's degree as a family nurse practitioner. Doing so would not only increase her earning potential but would open doors to a wider variety of jobs and allow her greater flexibility in future employment.

The challenge, of course, was not just financial. By this time, Aliza and her husband had three children, and choosing to put them in day care during Aliza's schooling was a real drain on their family budget. She noted that women who have children in day care are usually out earning money—but she was *spending it* going to school. Had she not been a recipient of the Ohio State Critical Difference for Women Re-Entry Scholarship, fulfilling her dreams would have presented tremendous difficulties for her family.

But the gift that came from Longaberger made all the difference. Aliza graduated as a Buckeye in 2006 and is now holding three separate part-time jobs in Ohio. She's the proud mother of four children now, all six years old and younger, all of whom have seen her fight to improve herself and enhance her education. She's grateful for the way she's been able to "cobble together" her employment opportunities so that she can still be home with her kids—all the while modeling the tenacity and fortitude she once saw in her own mother long ago.

Longaberger cares about women like Aliza, as well as those who have not known the love of family or the care of a supportive spouse. We have made very significant contributions to domestic violence shelters in the East Central and Southeast regions of Ohio.

We continue to support Mid-Ohio food banks through our Hunger Initiatives Program, which helps to disperse needed canned goods and personal items to food pantries throughout our area. We have also worked with pride to spearhead literacy, initiatives such as the "K-3 Reads" program, which supplies books and textbooks to small rural schools and community libraries across Ohio.

Because the Longaberger Foundation seeks to support and enhance our local community, we recently offered a grant to help the Miracle League of Muskingum County build a completely barrier-free, handicap-accessible baseball field. This project, led by Caribeth Legats, makes it possible for over 100 children and adults with special needs to play baseball in a supportive and celebratory environment. Caribeth shared with me how joyful her athletes are to play under the lights on spring evenings, hearing their names announced over a loudspeaker when they step up to the plate. The Miracle League helps to make baseball a *true* national pastime by extending the possibilities to those who are autistic, blind, in wheelchairs, using walkers, or living with other disabilities.

Furthermore, as an environmentalist, I was thrilled to hear that Caribeth garnered an additional outside grant of $100,000 from the Ohio Department of Natural Resources if her group would commit to using recycled *OHIO* tires to construct the rubber surface of the playing field. Can you believe that the efforts of the Miracle League Program helped to recycle *157,000 pounds of Ohio tires?* That's fantastic! It's so incredibly gratifying for me to be a part of a worthy project that then goes above and beyond by demonstrating stewardship to the earth while caring for others.

According to the latest available U.S. numbers, there are over 8,900 disabled children in the southeast portion of Ohio alone. Longaberger is delighted to have had a role in making summer more fun for all those who enjoy this ball field.

In truth, the work we do at the Longaberger Foundation is an extension of the love and gratitude we feel inside for all individuals, and in particular, for our statesmen, women, and children who hold a special place in our hearts. We understand our unique position to give financially, and it is our distinct pleasure to do so.

Perhaps reading these stories prompts you to consider your own giving. I've heard it said before that if your finances were exposed to the world, your priorities would suddenly become very obvious. Clearly, we spend our money on things we value or view as important. If that were to happen, what would we learn about you? Where are your priorities?

Maybe your honest answer would be that you're just trying to pay the bills—attempting to make ends meet in a fickle economy. If so, perhaps the best giving you can do right now is donating a few canned goods to your local food bank or volunteering your time at a women's shelter near your home. Don't diminish or undermine the importance of those gifts! Every little bit helps to ease the journey of someone who would otherwise struggle alone.

Perhaps an honest answer to that question would be that you enjoy frequenting Macy's or the Gap; maybe that's a priority for you right now. While a day at the mall is a fun diversion, don't let it blind you to the needs of others in your own community. Make it a point to decide what causes are important to you, and then give as you are able.

While it's true that not everyone has the resources of a foundation at their fingertips, everyone has the ability to make a difference.

I hope you'll do your part to help someone special in your world. Remind them that your love and care are not merely empty words.

Show them that they are a priority.

Part 9
Gratitude

35 Remembering to Say "Thank You"

Important People, Important Moments

Walking the five blocks to Marsha's house was best done with some imagination. Rather than merely taking the sidewalk or hopping on my bike, which would have been much too expected and mundane, Marsha and I used the railroad tracks as a topographic map that linked our homes like two points on a connect-the-dots game. We balanced like circus performers on the worn metal tracks slicing through Dresden, drawing lot lines across our backyards, holding our small Ohio homes at bay.

Marsha and I had been friends since we graduated kindergarten together. And that day, as I placed one 17-year-old foot in front of another, I realized that time had only strengthened us, adding lines to the face of our friendship story. What I didn't know was that my compassion for other people would be largely impacted by what was going on inside Marsha's house.

On that warm day after school, feet wobbling me toward her home, I rapped the back door and was greeted by Marsha's mother, Mrs. Myers.

"Well hello, Tami! It's good to see you! Come on in." She quickly wiped her floured hands on the stained apron tied around her waist and pushed the screen door open in what seemed like one fluid motion. The cacophony of children and dinner pots clanging reminded me that it was not just Marsha and her four siblings living there: It was Marsha, her siblings, *and several foster children* who occupied the home.

Marsha swooped into the kitchen and grabbed a cookie from the rows that were cooling on sheets of parchment paper by the stove.

"Hey, Tami—let me just get Felicia's shoes on and we'll be ready to go. Have a cookie—my mom's are the best!"

Felicia was one of the foster kids living with the Myers, and one to whom we both had grown particularly attached. She was a beautiful little girl with thick ringlets and chocolate eyes that peeked out from beneath impossibly long lashes. Pudgy hands dimpled at the base of her smooth fingers, cheeks overtaking her round face.

It never occurred to me to notice that her skin was darker than mine—or that this even mattered.

With Felicia tucked safely in her stroller, Marsha and I set out for town. At that age going anywhere was a treat, and taking Felicia with us made it all the more special. Her laughter was contagious, and her sweet disposition, positively endearing.

But what I started to notice that afternoon in 1978 was that not *everyone* thought it was endearing to see two high school seniors toting around a child—much less *a child of a different race.* As we walked through the local department store, eyes narrowed, glaring unabashedly. Heads turned. Eyebrows rose in judgment.

I laughed nervously. And kept walking.

What I understood in that important moment was that the scary, awful, pit-in-your-stomach kind of racism *was being directed at me* for investing in the life of another human being. What I understood in that moment was that some people still look with their eyes instead of loving with their hearts. And the memory of it all is burned into me like the singe of a branding iron still orange with heat.

What I *learned* in that moment was compassion. Compassion, first of all for Felicia; for a child without a home. For a child who would be loved, smothered with kisses, and then relinquished at the word of any number of state officials.

Compassion for Anna and Gary Myers, who grew attached and began to love these children. Compassion for the mothers who moved behind the scenes like ghosts, surrendering their children to the system, forfeiting hopes and dreams because of some unnamed trauma that had erupted in their own lives.

And I was also somehow softened toward the ones who snickered and jeered. The ones who wouldn't hold my gaze or open their hearts to love and acceptance, clinging instead to ignorance and blind judgment. I know now that they deserve a measure of compassion, too.

That experience was a powerful one for me; I felt judged by strangers in my own town. By neighbors and shopkeepers. By my father's peers. It reminded me that sometimes showing love is hard, or at least uncomfortable. But that it matters. It mattered to a little girl named Felicia, and so it matters to me.

Marsha and I are friends to this day, 40-something years after kindergarten, and more than a score since high school. She still works for The Longaberger Company; and we still think of Felicia.

We think of Felicia and the thousands of other children like her who have gone through the foster system and have never truly had their own bed or their own room. We think of children who will not see a Christmas stocking embroidered with their name hanging above a crackling fireplace this holiday season. And who will walk into town and be greeted by the sideways glances of strangers.

I am so grateful for the lesson I learned in Dresden years ago. It's a daily reminder of our call to rise above ugly assumptions and petty differences. It reminds me to extend my arms in love to those the world deems unlovable or undesirable.

It reminds me that the world needs a few more people with hearts like Anna Myers's.

I'm determined to be one of them.

Will you?

36 A Posture of Gratitude

How I Live with a Grateful Heart

Dear Matthew, . . .

My pen stops. And so does my heart.

I try to steady myself, to not smear ink across fresh paper.

Instead, it's my mascara that smears in puddles of fresh tears.

Never are the words so difficult to write as they are on the sacred handful of days tucked between Christmas and New Year's Day, sheltered from harsh December snows by two epic holidays and the warmth of a vacation at home.

One of the most emotionally difficult things I've done to live out a posture of gratitude is to write letters to my children in that wintry snatch of time; letters that they will not receive until I'm gone. And until the publication of this book, letters they never even knew I was writing.

Sitting down to ponder what the future might look like for Claire and Matthew, I scrawl my thoughts mingled with words of encouragement, showering blessings on their lives.

I attempt to impart the kind of motherly wisdom that comes with age and loving deeply. I strive to remind them of who they are, and I ask them who they've become. I wonder about their journeys, about their homes and loves and children. And I remind them of me and how much I'm missing them. How much I'm wishing I could be there to see them mother and father their own little ones.

I tell them how immensely grateful I am to have been their mother. I describe the immeasurable joy they brought into my years on earth; how they colored each of my days with dazzling beauty and joy. I talk to each of them as only a mother can, knowing them intimately as only a mother can.

And as heartbreaking as it is to write these words to a living child, I think of how profoundly touching it would be if I were to come upon a letter from my father or my Grandma Bonnie, both gone now. I imagine Claire and Matthew going through my papers, leafing through personal effects and discovering a sealed envelope. Then two. Then three. And another and another and another.

And it makes me grateful for the years I have with them right now. It makes me appreciate these minutes and hours and days so much more when I place them in the context of my unavoidable future absence.

I take the time to think about my children and the way they've grown and changed and matured over the space of a year. I peel them back, removing secret layers and getting to the core of who they are: a young man, a young woman, my very life, my very heart, beating outside my chest.

Though it's a crushing exercise, it's one that renews a posture of gratitude for a new year—a new year of hopes and dreams spread out like untouched canvas across the calendar of our lives.

Today the calendar reads May, and my peonies are in bloom. Today peonies are informing my posture of gratitude.

This morning, I wandered past the vividly green bushes in my backyard and ventured into the woods beyond the view of my kitchen windows. That's where I happened upon my gift: a weighty, seven-inch-wide peony bursting with color. I picked some May apples and a fern frond to keep it company, marveling at its exquisite beauty.

Holding it close to my face and breathing in its life and grace, I had another reason to smile. I crossed the threshold to my kitchen and slipped it into a vase with its garden friends. It is flamboyant and brilliantly pink. If I took another step closer or bent farther down, I'm certain I could hear a melody coming from its simplicity and perfection.

This simple seven-inch peony makes me grateful. It's not a $100 arrangement. It's not professionally done in a studio and then delivered to my doorstep. Better yet, it's from my yard. And its loveliness is a free gift.

Those moments of unity with nature make me incredibly grateful.

I'm thankful for slender green stems and the exact color of each petal—for the explosion of life supported by leaves and roots and the dirt of home.

I'm grateful for the simple things; for my children and the years I have with them. For the gifts of our earth. For peonies in a vase with ferns. I'm grateful for all of life, because now more than ever, I realize it's all a gift—if we only have eyes to see it.

37 "How Can I Say Thanks?"

A Consultant's Gratitude

Sometimes it's hard for me to share stories of consultants' gratitude for the Longaberger opportunity because it feels like braggadocio. I've never been totally comfortable with the limelight; I'd much rather be behind the scenes, working to make things seem effortlessly successful.

Regardless of all my years with the company, some things are still a bit foreign to me. I'm used to them—and thankful for them—in the way that I imagine an American might, over time, get used to driving a car in London. She might drive decades through the tight city streets, winding past red phone booths and Harrod's nearly every day. She may even appreciate the car she maneuvers and her ability to drive in a lovely area so full of history. Yet when she's back at home snuggled up under the family quilt next to a smoldering fire, watching rain slide down the windowpanes, she will tell you: Yes. I drive in London. Have for years. Don't rightly remember the last time I *haven't been driving in London*. But it's not *quite* as second nature—not completely as automatic and inherent—as driving in the States; on the *right side of the road*.

Recently, I've been spending some time listening to consultants tell their stories. Some come from men and women who have been with the company for a long time, while others come from relatively new folks. Yet despite their differences, an overarching theme seems to be emerging. Without fail, they gush about how deeply they love this company; how it afforded them new opportunities and helped them to achieve more than they ever dreamed possible. They tell me how much Longaberger feels like a family to them. And inevitably, they share how they view me, oftentimes as a key part of that family, and thereby, as a key part of the story they treasure.

One of the people whose story I've recently heard is a woman named Cheryl Benoodt. Cheryl and I have been friends for a long time; she had a close friendship with my Dad and has at times felt more like a surrogate big sister than a colleague. Cheryl started her Longaberger business when her daughter went to college, expecting only to dabble in it, make a little extra money, enjoy new friendships, and nothing more.

Now, having been with the company for 24 years, Cheryl admits that she has accomplished more than she ever expected. She's occupied the number-one national sales spot for several years, claimed the number-two position for many more, and received the illustrious "Spirit of Longaberger" Award in 1999.

Despite her accolades and prominence at Longaberger, the flip side of Cheryl's coin has been marked by difficulty. And while it may be true that everyone goes through challenging times, suffers heartbreak, and wrestles to break free from the weight of life, it seems that Cheryl has been wading in more than her share of grief and struggle for some time.

I remember when Cheryl's Dad had a stroke and became paralyzed, living out his days in a nursing home. She would drive to be by his side, a loyal daughter and only child, arriving in the evening to feed him dinner and help care for him as best she could. Along with the help of a supportive and attentive stepmother, Cheryl willingly tended to her father during those last gloomy months, walking through days and evenings with a smile and positive attitude.

While Cheryl worked to sustain her father, news of my own Dad's death in March 1999 reached her, and she was wracked with the sadness that comes from losing a dear friend. As though tearing the scab off a fresh wound, Cheryl again dove into the stinging pool of mourning when her father died, just months later, in August of the same year. We called each other, talked, laughed, and cried. We understood one another. We could relate, and empathize. And through it all, we grew closer.

At home, Cheryl leaned heavily on her husband, Denny, and the security of their close relationship. Having married young, Cheryl looked to Denny as her lifeline. Her confidant. Her lover and best friend. As empty nesters with one daughter living states away, they cherished the time they had together, with Denny often helping Cheryl with her Longaberger business and accompanying her to Ohio for our annual convention, The Bee. They enjoyed the kind of marriage that, to the outside world, seemed enviable. Their life was marked by easy banter, filled with knowing looks of quiet understanding and mutual respect. The kind of love that, if not perfect, was *truly special.*

Denny had been diagnosed with cancer as a young man, and though it had long gone into remission, he spent much of the time following his ordeal battling heart issues. In 1994, he withstood quintuple-bypass surgery to repair his failing heart and strengthen it for what doctors and his family hoped would be years to come. Then, in November 2002, after tests and waiting and watching, Denny decided to undergo a routine surgery to have a heart valve put in.

With her husband tucked safely into the gurney, Cheryl and five of her closest Longaberger friends planted themselves in the hospital waiting room to see him emerge stronger, healthier—his old vibrant self.

But when the nurse came out to give a status report, Cheryl could feel the color drain from her face. Despite words meant to reassure, her body betrayed her: hands grew clammy, stomach churned, and eyes welled. Certainly there was no real reason to worry, her friends told her—after all, what was it the nurse said? *"We're having a few minor problems, but nothing serious. We did install a pacemaker to get him regulated in the meantime."*

Women surrounded her like a tomato cage in a spring garden, giving her something strong to lean on, something strong to support the bending that would come under this kind of devilish weight.

But with or without friends reassuring her, Cheryl felt an uneasiness, a sinister storm brewing—one that began to rage and beat against her insides when she first glimpsed the man in scrubs walking toward her from the shadows at the far end of the hallway. She felt her head shaking, felt her knees become gelatinous caverns midway through her stretch of legs.

It took a moment for the doctor's words to register. The room felt claustrophobic and suddenly tiny—clothing became restrictive, her chest crushed under the weight of cotton, gasping for air as buttons sucked life from her lungs.

Denny had died—at the age of 55.

When I received word of the news, my spirit deflated like air pouring unstoppably from a limp balloon. Having known Denny personally, I felt the prickle of my own pain mingling with the tsunami-sized bereavement that was surely engulfing Cheryl. I sent word that I was on my way.

And I was.

I got on a plane two days later and flew to Illinois for the funeral. Sitting there amidst the rows of friends and family, people who had known Denny for years and years—for a lifetime, really—I couldn't have felt prouder to have known him myself. And I couldn't have been more glad to have been there *for* Cheryl and *with* Cheryl; sharing in her grief, feeling her loss, and understanding a bit of the undertow pulling at her heels.

After listening to the eulogies and watching folks file to the back of the room, I went up to Cheryl and let my arms envelop her. Sobbing, her body shuddered against mine, and I felt such love for her. For my friend. For part of our family.

"Cheryl," I began, "I knew Denny was a great guy. I knew he was a fabulous cattleman—that he had a tremendous business. But I just didn't realize *how* wonderful he was or *all* that he had accomplished. I felt so good inside that I knew him as well as I did."

Cheryl would later tell me that it wasn't just me who helped tether her during those moments of darkness and loneliness; it was her *entire Longaberger family*. The cards, notes, letters, phone calls; friends sitting with her. The calming awareness of the presence of others. She explained how her business gave her new goals, kept her occupied, connected her with other women, and provided a community that stretched well beyond the limits of her town.

Cheryl is still one of our top sellers today. She continues to exude her positive energy and warm personality while working her business, despite spending days at the hospital caring for her ailing mother. She is consistently building her team and scheduling parties, despite the realization that others may soon need her help and care. For her, the flexibility and income that her role at Longaberger provides have enabled her to make a life for herself while still *living* life on her own terms. And the *family* that we all feel a part of makes living life *a joy.*

When I asked Cheryl what it is about Longaberger that keeps her working at a time when many others would retire, she just chuckles and whispers, *"I love it."* She recalls story after story of great memories we've shared: of winning 12 silver platters of shoes delivered by 12 handsome men one year at The Bee, something we planned especially for her. She remembers visiting my home and spending the night with other consultants, and breathes the memory of visiting my father's grave with me. She confesses:

> *Longaberger has given me the opportunity to improve myself. I always knew I was capable, but Longaberger has a way of drawing out the best—something bigger and brighter. It has made me better. How can I say thank you for so many blessings? I am eternally grateful.*

Cheryl doesn't dwell on the hardships life has handed her. Rather, she recalls her gratitude and recounts the many ways that her life has been changed. And if, by some grand design, I—and Longaberger as a whole—have played a role in the story of her life—if we had a hand in the story of her gratitude, well, then, it is *me* who is blessed.

I am the one who is grateful.

38 Grateful to You

People Make Longaberger What It Is

When I look back on my life—this amazing, crazy life of wonderful experiences and unexpected opportunities—I am struck most by the profound impact that people have made on me and on my journey with Longaberger.

I have been touched by hundreds of people and been enriched by tens of thousands of brief interactions that remind me of how loved I am. I am humbled to hear of how I may have made a difference in his life or her life *or your life*—because I am too often blinded by the difference that you all have made in mine.

I could compose lengthy lists of the people for whom I am grateful. For my family, first, and my children. For the employees, past and present, who give so much of themselves at The Longaberger Company, giving birth to creativity and new design. For the tens of thousands of Home Consultants and their families who work to make their Longaberger businesses successful each day.

But in truth, it is *more* than the one-on-one relationships I have with our employees or consultants—although those are, of course, dear and priceless and precious to me. What I am so grateful for and so incredibly appreciative of is the *collective* effects that *all these relationships* have had on my heart—relationships from *all walks of life.*

I am grateful for women and men who are struggling with life and find Longaberger when they've nearly reached the ends of their ropes. I cheer for them as they turn around, climbing back out of the darkness with new friends at their sides. I am grateful for the way they inspire me to do more and to do better. I praise them for how they inspire and encourage a whole new generation of young people who desperately need strong role models and loving voices in their lives.

I am grateful for the lawyers and teachers I've met; for young and old, healthy and ailing. For those who hold divergent points of view, who enlighten me with new perspectives, who challenge me to see the world through a different lens. I am thankful to have met people from all over this world, from small villages and large metropolitan areas; people with opposing religious viewpoints and contrasting political ideals.

All of them have a place in my history. I approach each of them with a heart bent toward listening and understanding, toward learning something valuable from that singular encounter. *And being present in that moment makes me grateful.*

When all the stories are woven together, I pause and realize: *We are all bound together by a common thread called Longaberger.* Together, we make up the DNA of this company. We have all been grafted in and provide life and love to each other like a hardy vine sprouting buds in summer, taking in the rain and helping one another become greener and more beautiful.

And so each day, as I flip through snapshots in my mind, I see your faces—and theirs—and I am grateful. I remember your stories and know your struggles and hear your voices in my heart. And I am grateful.

Each day, as I look into the faces of my children, or gaze upon the beauty of a bird in flight or a flower in bloom, I am grateful. As I weave my own dreams and consider my future and what may lie in store, I am grateful.

Thank you for allowing yourself to be included in this stunning, extraordinary tapestry. Thank you for giving of yourself in so many ways; for stretching and bending and changing along with me. *Thank you for joining me on the journey.*

You, and so many others like you, make it effortless for me to find the joy of work . . . and the love of life.

INDEX

Tami and her two children, Claire and Matthew, pictured here in 2010.